STUDENTS AND STAFFORD LOANS

IMPACT ON BORROWING AND EDUCATION EXPENSES

EDUCATION IN A COMPETITIVE AND GLOBALIZING WORLD

Additional books in this series can be found on Nova's website under the Series tab.

Additional e-books in this series can be found on Nova's website under the e-book tab.

STUDENTS AND STAFFORD LOANS

IMPACT ON BORROWING AND EDUCATION EXPENSES

DAPHNE ROLLINS
EDITOR

New York

NOTICE TO THE READER

Library of Congress Cataloging-in-Publication Data

ISBN: 978-1-63321-126-1

Published by Nova Science Publishers, Inc. † New York

CONTENTS

PREFACE

A college education can increase the choices and opportunities available to individuals, but high college tuition rates have prompted concerns that a college education may be an unattainable goal for some. To help students finance their education, Congress passed a law that raised the ceiling on the amount students can borrow under the federal Stafford Loan Program. This book examines the extent to which, if any, the Stafford loan limit increases affected tuition, fees and room and board prices at institutions of higher education; and the trends in private student loan borrowing since the loan limits took effect.

Chapter 1 - A college education can increase the choices and opportunities available to individuals, but high college tuition rates have prompted concerns that a college education may be an unattainable goal for some. To help students finance their education, Congress passed a law that raised the ceiling on the amount students can borrow under the federal Stafford Loan Program (referred to in the law as "loan limits"). The Ensuring Continued Access to Student Loans Act of 2008 mandated a series of GAO reports over a 5 year period assessing the impact of these increases in the loan limits on tuition and other expenses and on private student loan borrowing.

For this final report, GAO examined: (1) the extent to which, if any, the Stafford loan limit increases affected tuition, fees and room and board prices at institutions of higher education; and (2) the trends in private student loan borrowing since the loan limits took effect. GAO developed a statistical model to explore whether the loan limit increases in academic years 2007-08 and 2008-09 had an impact on college prices in subsequent years. GAO analyzed data from the Department of Education (Education) and the Consumer Financial Protection Bureau (CFPB), and interviewed officials from eight higher education institutions that represented a mix of college sectors in different regions of the country, three of the largest private student lenders, federal officials, and subject matter specialists.

Chapter 2 - Report of the United States Government Accountability Office on Federal Student Loans: Patterns in Tuition, Enrollment, and Federal Stafford Loan Borrowing Up to the 2007-08 Loan Limit Increase.

Chapter 3 - In recent decades, students and families increasingly have turned to loans to help pay for postsecondary education, and most undergraduates who borrow to finance their education use the federal loan programs. Federal loans include Stafford, Perkins, and Parent PLUS loans, with the Stafford loan program being the largest, at a total of $35 billion borrowed by undergraduates in 2007–08. As this report will show, in 1989–90, some 27 percent of all undergraduates had taken out a federal Stafford loan at some point during their enrollment in postsecondary education, while in 2007–08, this proportion was 46 percent. In addition, the average cumulative amount among all undergraduate borrowers was higher, even after adjusting for inflation. In 2007–08, the average cumulative Stafford loan amount was $10,300, compared with $7,200 (in constant 2007 dollars) in 1989–90.

In: Students and Stafford Loans
Editor: Daphne Rollins

ISBN: 978-1-63321-126-1
© 2014 Nova Science Publishers, Inc.

Chapter 1

FEDERAL STUDENT LOANS: IMPACT OF LOAN LIMIT INCREASES ON COLLEGE PRICES IS DIFFICULT TO DISCERN[*]

United States Government Accountability Office

WHY GAO DID THIS STUDY

A college education can increase the choices and opportunities available to individuals, but high college tuition rates have prompted concerns that a college education may be an unattainable goal for some. To help students finance their education, Congress passed a law that raised the ceiling on the amount students can borrow under the federal Stafford Loan Program (referred to in the law as "loan limits"). The Ensuring Continued Access to Student Loans Act of 2008 mandated a series of GAO reports over a 5 year period assessing the impact of these increases in the loan limits on tuition and other expenses and on private student loan borrowing.

For this final report, GAO examined: (1) the extent to which, if any, the Stafford loan limit increases affected tuition, fees and room and board prices at institutions of higher education; and (2) the trends in private student loan borrowing since the loan limits took effect. GAO developed a statistical model to explore whether the loan limit increases in academic years 2007-08 and

---

[*] This is an edited, reformatted and augmented version of the United States Government Accountability Office publication, GAO-14-7, dated February 2014.

2008-09 had an impact on college prices in subsequent years. GAO analyzed data from the Department of Education (Education) and the Consumer Financial Protection Bureau (CFPB), and interviewed officials from eight higher education institutions that represented a mix of college sectors in different regions of the country, three of the largest private student lenders, federal officials, and subject matter specialists.

WHAT GAO RECOMMENDS

GAO makes no recommendations in this report. Education and CFPB had no comments.

WHAT GAO FOUND

For more than a decade, college prices have been rising consistently and have continued to rise at a gradual pace after the Stafford loan limit increases were enacted in 2008 and 2009. However, it is difficult to determine if a direct relationship exists between increases in college prices and the Stafford loan limit increases because of the confluence of many other factors that occurred around the time the loan limit increases took effect. Specifically, when the loan limit increases took effect, the nation was in a recession, which created one of the most tumultuous and complex economic environments in recent history. GAO's analysis found that the economic effects of the recession, which affected families' employment, income, and net worth make it difficult to isolate the impact the recession had on students' decisions to borrow money to finance college expenses versus the impact of the loan limit increases. Further, federal, state, and institutional aid available to students also increased significantly around the same time the loan limit increases went into effect. It is difficult to determine the extent to which the increased availability of this financial aid influenced the decisions of students on whether and how much money they should borrow versus the availability of increased loan limits. Conversely, GAO's analysis shows that even though college prices continued to increase at a gradual pace over the last decade as well as after the loan limits increased, enrollment, which can be sensitive to price increases, also generally continued to grow across both public and private institutions and in all regions of the country.

Around the time that the loan limit increases took effect, the number of students taking out private education loans decreased across all types of institutions; lenders were making fewer loans and students borrowed less. Specifically, before the loan limit increases, the number of students borrowing private loans for academic year 2007-08 was about 2.8 million; after the limits went into effect the number dropped by over 50 percent to about 1.3 million for academic year 2011-12. Similarly, the average amount of money that students borrowed from private student loans decreased by about 17 percent after the loan limits went into effect. For example, for academic year 2007-08 students' private student loans averaged about $7,048 and for academic year 2011-12 this had dropped to about $5,870. According to the federal and institutional officials as well as financial lending experts that GAO spoke with, many factors may explain the changed private loan landscape. For example, these officials and experts noted that:

- lenders tightened lending criteria—such as requiring higher credit scores and co-signers—making it more difficult to obtain these loans;
- Congress enacted new protections to raise students' awareness about private loans, including disclosures of loan rates and terms; and
- colleges took steps to help students find alternatives to private borrowing and reduce reliance on private loans, such as increasing institutional aid and providing financial literacy counseling to help inform students about their federal assistance options.

ABBREVIATIONS

CFPB	Consumer Financial Protection Bureau
Education	Department of Education
EFC	Expected Family Contribution
FFEL	Federal Family Education Loan Program
FICO	Fair Isaac Corporation credit score
FRED	Federal Reserve Economic Data
HEOA	Higher Education Opportunity Act
IPEDS	Integrated Postsecondary Education Data System
NPSAS	National Postsecondary Student Aid Study
PLUS	Federal Parent Loans for Undergraduate Students
TILA	Truth in Lending Act

February 18, 2014

The Honorable Tom Harkin
Chairman
The Honorable Lamar Alexander
Ranking Member
Committee on Health, Education, Labor and Pensions
United States Senate

The Honorable John Kline
Chairman
The Honorable George Miller
Ranking Member
Committee on Education and the Workforce
House of Representatives

A college education can increase the choices and opportunities available to individuals, but rising costs have prompted concerns that a college education may be an unattainable goal for some. To help students afford the rising cost of college, Congress passed a law that raised the ceiling on the amount individual students can borrow (referred to in the law as "loan limits") under the federal Stafford Loan Program. Although increasing federal loan limits would give students more resources to pay for college, there is also concern that the availability of this additional resource might present an incentive for colleges to charge students more. At the same time, this opportunity to borrow more federal loan money might affect students' private loan borrowing, which sometimes may have significantly higher interest rates and default rates than federal student loans. The Ensuring Continued Access to Student Loans Act of 2008[1] mandated GAO to conduct a series of reports over 5 years assessing the impact of loan limit increases on tuition and other expenses and on private loan borrowing.[2] This is our final study in response to this mandate. For this study, we addressed (1) to what extent, if any, did the Stafford loan limit increases affect tuition, fees and room and board prices at institutions of higher education; and (2) what have been the trends in private student loan borrowing since the loan limits took effect?

To determine the extent, if any, to which Stafford loan limit increases affected college prices, we developed a panel regression model—a statistical method where we collected data over time for the same colleges to estimate possible relationships among certain variables, controlling for the effects of other variables—to examine the impact of Stafford loan limit increases on tuition, fees, and room and board prices at institutions of higher education.[3] In order to isolate the effect of loan limits from other factors that may influence tuition and other college prices, we controlled for factors such as college revenue from state appropriations or endowments, and economic variables such as the state-level unemployment rate. To determine if there were actual changes in the amounts students borrowed in federal Stafford loans before and after the loan limits took effect, we supplemented the findings of our panel regression model with the most recent data available from the National Postsecondary Student Aid Study (NPSAS) database (academic years 2003-04, 2007-08 and 2011-12), and trend data (academic years 1999-2000 through 2011-12) for all Title IV-eligible,[4] degree-granting institutions of higher education from the Department of Education's (Education) Integrated Postsecondary Education Data System (IPEDS). Using these data, we examined differences in tuition trends among four education institutional sectors—nonprofit,[5] for-profit, public 2-year, and public 4-year colleges—and geographic regions.[6] For public 2-year and public 4-year colleges, we also reviewed the annual tuition for both in-state and out-of- state students. For both the IPEDS trend data and panel regression model data, we analyzed data for undergraduate students—the majority of college students—to measure the effect of the two separate loan limit increases.[7] To provide examples of the role, if any, the loan limit increases played in how colleges set prices, we supplemented these data with interviews from college officials at eight institutions. We selected a nonprobability sample of institutions to obtain a mix of each major sector of higher education, regions, amount of federal aid received, enrollment sizes, admission selectivity levels, and prices of tuition and related fees. Although we cannot generalize information from these interviews to the broader higher education landscape, we believe that the information from these eight institutions provides insight into colleges' perspectives about the role of loan limit increases on college prices and federal and private student loan borrowing trends. In addition, we interviewed federal officials and subject matter specialists, including academic researchers.

With respect to our second objective, we analyzed the trends in private student borrowing because comprehensive data from private lenders were not available to assess the impact of loan limit increases on private student borrowing, and data from individual lenders are proprietary. To determine trends in private student loan borrowing since the loan limit increases took effect, we reviewed aggregate trend data from calendar years 2005 through 2011 for nine major private student lenders reported in a 2012 study by the

Consumer Financial Protection Bureau (CFPB) and Education.[8] To obtain additional information about trends after the loan limit increases, we supplemented the CFPB study data with analyses of Education's IPEDS data (academic years 1999-2000 through 2011-12) and NPSAS data (academic years 2003-04, 2007-08, and 2011-12) about private student loan usage and undergraduate borrowing. We also reviewed federal laws and regulations that have affected the private lending market. We interviewed officials from the same eight institutions we selected for research objective 1 and asked about private student loan borrowing. We also interviewed three of the largest private student lenders who participated in the CFPB study about the private student loan industry, borrowing trends, and the extent to which the increased Stafford loan limits affected private student loan borrowing. Finally, we interviewed representatives from relevant professional associations, federal officials, and subject matter specialists, including academic researchers. See appendix I for our detailed scope and methodology and appendix II for details on our panel regression model.

We determined that the IPEDS and NPSAS data are sufficiently reliable for the purposes of this report by testing them for accuracy and completeness, and by reviewing documentation about the systems used to produce the data. Unless otherwise noted, all percentage estimates from NPSAS have 95 percent confidence intervals that are within 8 percent of the estimate itself. Further, all NPSAS dollar estimates have 95 percent confidence intervals that are within 8 percentage points of the estimate itself. We conducted this performance audit from December 2012 to February 2014 in accordance with generally accepted government auditing standards. Those standards require that we plan and perform the audit to obtain sufficient, appropriate evidence to provide a reasonable basis for our findings and conclusions based on our audit objectives. We believe that the evidence we obtained provides a reasonable basis for our findings and conclusions based on our audit objectives.

BACKGROUND

To help students pay for college, several forms of financial aid are available through federal, state, institutional, and private sources, as shown in table 1.

Table 1. Major Aid Programs for Undergraduate Students (Aggregate Spending), Academic Years 2006-07, 2008-09, and 2011-12

(millions of academic year 2012 constant dollars)			
	2006-07	**2008-09**	**2011-12**
Federal Stafford Loans	55,573	76,505	89,607
Federal Pell Grants	14,430	19,051	34,048
Federal Parent Loans for Undergraduate Students (PLUS)	11,507	12,514	18,931
Federal tax benefits[a]	7,410	11,160	20,280
Federal veterans grants[b]	3,710	4,358	11,007
State grants	8,535	8,749	9,532
Institutional grants	29,510	32,310	42,650
State and Institution loans	2,360	1,660	1,690
Private student loans	21,390	10,730	6,440

Source: College Board, Trends in Student Aid 2013.

[a] The latest available data for federal education tax benefits are for calendar year 2011. Estimates for 2011-2012 are based on these data, and only include the Hope, Lifetime Learning, and American Opportunity tax credits.

[b] Federal veterans grants include payments for postsecondary education and training to veterans and their dependents, including the Post-9/11 Veterans Educational Assistance program effective for academic year 2009-10 (38 U.S.C. §§ 3301-3324) and all programs established earlier. Some of these funds also cover living expenses and other education-related costs. The Iraq and Afghanistan Service Grants program was effective in academic year 2010-11. This program provides non-need- based grants for students whose parent or guardian was a member of the Armed Forces who died in Iraq or Afghanistan as a result of performing military service after Sept. 11, 2001. 20 U.S.C. § 1070h.

In academic year 2011-12, about 70 percent of the undergraduate students attending college borrowed money from federal or private lenders. Before 2010, federal Stafford Loans and PLUS Loans were part of the Federal Family Education Loan (FFEL) Program as well as the William D. Ford Federal Direct Loan (Direct Loan) Program. Under the FFEL Program, private lenders made federally-guaranteed student loans to parents and students. The Student Aid and Fiscal Responsibility Act of 2009, enacted as a part of the Health Care and Education Reconciliation Act of 2010, terminated the authority to make or insure new FFEL loans after June 30, 2010.[9] At the time, there was concern that paying banks to act as middlemen for student lending was adding to the cost of student borrowing. A Congressional Budget Office study estimated that the government would save over $85 billion over 10 years if it did the direct lending itself.[10] Starting July 1, 2010 all Stafford and PLUS loans are originated and disbursed directly from the Department of Education under the Federal Direct Loan Program. FFEL Program loans disbursed before July 1, 2010 continue to be serviced according to the terms and conditions of the FFEL Program master promissory note the borrowers signed when they obtained the loan.

The Stafford Loan program is the largest source of federal financial aid available to postsecondary students.[11] In academic year 2011-12, 35 percent of undergraduate students participated in the program, which provided an estimated $89.6 billion to eligible students through subsidized and unsubsidized loans.[12] The federal government pays the interest on subsidized loans while students are in school, and students must have a financial need as determined under federal law to qualify for this type of loan. Each student's financial aid need is determined by subtracting the student's expected family contribution (EFC) and certain other estimated financial assistance from the total price of attendance.[13] Regardless of their financial need, students can borrow unsubsidized loans to pay for educational expenses and are responsible for paying back any interest that accrues on the loan. A student may be eligible to receive both subsidized and unsubsidized loans, which are generally referred to as a combined loan.

To help students and their families pay for the rising cost of college, Congress first passed a law that raised Stafford loan limits for first-and second-year undergraduate students as well as for graduate and professional students in academic year 2007-08,[14] and subsequently for all qualified undergraduate students receiving unsubsidized or combined Stafford loans in academic year 2008-09 (see table 2).[15]

Students whose financial need is not fully met by federal assistance and the school's own resources (school grants and loans, called institutional aid) may turn to private lenders for college funding. While the private student loan market is dominated by traditional financial institutions such as banks, a variety of other private student lenders exist. Specifically, in addition to the traditional banks, nonprofit lenders, many of which are affiliated with states and certain schools, have elected to fund or effectively guarantee loans.

Table 2. Statutory Stafford Loan Limits before and after the Increases: Comparison of Academic Years 2006-07, 2007-08, and 2008-09

Class level	Academic year	Subsidized loan	Unsubsidized loan	Combined total
Annual loan limits for dependent students				
1st Year	2006-07	$2,625	$2,625	$2,625
	2007-08	3,500	3,500	3,500
	2008-09	3,500	5,500	5,500
2nd Year	2006-07	3,500	3,500	3,500
	2007-08	4,500	4,500	4,500
	2008-09	4,500	6,500	6,500
Annual loan limits for independent students[a]				
1st Year	2006-07	2,625	6,625	6,625
	2007-08	3,500	7,500	7,500
	2008-09	3,500	9,500	9,500
2nd Year	2006-07	3,500	7,500	7,500
	2007-08	4,500	8,500	8,500
	2008-09	4,500	10,500	10,500

Source: GAO analysis of relevant federal laws.

[a] Students who are 24 years of age or older are considered independent. Younger students can also be classified as independent under certain circumstances, such as if they are married or are on active military duty.

ANY IMPACT OF INCREASES IN LOAN LIMITS ON RISING COLLEGE PRICES IS DIFFICULT TO DISCERN

For more than a decade, college prices have been rising consistently across most types of institutions of higher education and continued to rise after the Stafford loan limits increased, but it is difficult to establish if a direct relationship exists.[16] Numerous events that affected the economy likely influenced rising prices, which generally followed a consistent upward pattern across three commonly-used measures of college prices (see Figure 1).[17]

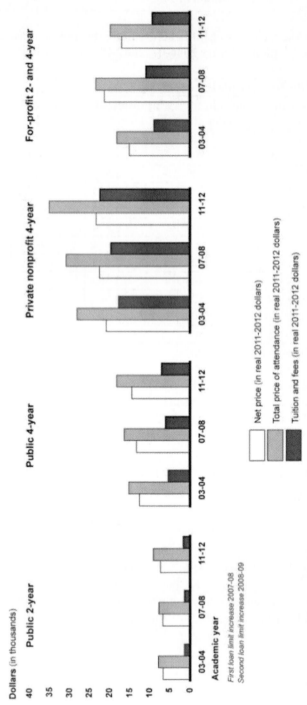

Source: GAO analysis of National Postsecondary Student Aid Study data.

Note: The tuition and fees data from the National Postsecondary Student Aid Study (NPSAS) displayed in this figure are lower than the tuition and fees data from the Integrated Postsecondary Education Data System (IPEDS) because the NPSAS data includes part-time students whereas the data from IPEDS displays data only for full-time undergraduates.

Figure 1. Common Measures of College Prices, Academic Years 2003-04, 2007-08, and 2011-12.

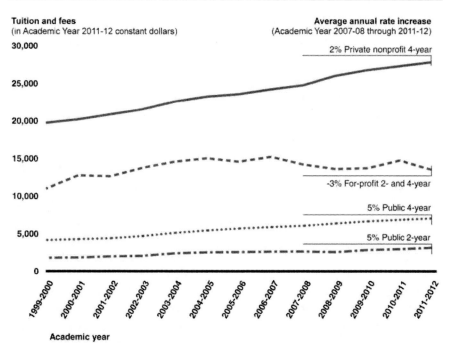

Tuition and fees
(in Academic Year 2011-12 constant dollars)

Average annual rate increase
(Academic Year 2007-08 through 2011-12)

2% Private nonprofit 4-year

-3% For-profit 2- and 4-year

5% Public 4-year

5% Public 2-year

Academic year

Source: GAO analysis of Integrated Postsecondary Education Data System data.
Note: The tuition and fees for public 2- year and public 4-year schools are for in-state
students.

Figure 2. Tuition and Required Fees, Academic Years 1999-2012, for Full-time
Undergraduate Students.

As figure 2 shows, the tuition and required fees that a typical student
would incur rose at an average annual rate of about 2 to 5 percent from
academic years 2007-08 through 2011-12, following a decade-long trend of
steady, consistent increases. The one exception to this pattern was at for-profit
2-and 4-year institutions, where prices decreased across all three measures
during that time (see Figure 1). That is, for academic years 2007-08 through
2011-12, the tuition and required fees decreased at an annual average rate of 3
percent (see Figure 2).[18]

This pattern of gradual increases in tuition and fees has generally persisted
across different regions of the United States, with higher overall annual rate
increases from academic years 2007-08 through 2011-12 in the Far West
region (average annual rate increase of 14 percent),[19] and lower increases in
the Great Lakes and Plains regions at 1 and 2 percent, respectively.[20]
Enrollment, which can be sensitive to college prices, was unaffected by

increases in college prices, and continued an upward trend as shown in figure 3, rising to about 18 million students in academic year 2011-12, with variations by region, student characteristics, and higher education sector. Further, over the last decade,[21] the cohort of college students who are 18-24 has grown substantially, with this population comprising about 42 percent of all college students in 2011. See Appendix III for additional data on college prices and enrollment.

Although college prices went up, we were unable to determine whether or not these increases resulted from the loan limit increases because of the interference of various economic factors occurring around the same time these loan limit increases went into effect. Specifically, when the loan limit increases went into effect, the nation was in a recession which created one of the most tumultuous and complex economic environments in recent history, affecting families' employment, income, and net worth (see Figure 4). As shown earlier, the availability and types of federal and institutional financial aid available to students increased around the time the new loan limits went into effect (see table 1), also making it difficult to discern any effect those loan limits may have had. For example, the dollar amounts of Federal PLUS loans, federal tax benefits, Pell grants, and federal veterans grants all increased. Further, the amounts of state and institutional grants and loans also increased, while the amounts of state appropriations for colleges and college endowments decreased.

Further, colleges appear to have responded to the economic crisis in ways that are difficult to capture in a model. We found some evidence of this in our discussion with selected college officials, who responded to the economic crisis in different ways. For example, officials at a private nonprofit 4-year institution said that despite declines in their endowments, they used their general operating and annual giving funds to provide more aid to students. In contrast, officials at one public 4-year college said that they set their tuition so that their students, the majority of whom qualified for federal Pell grants, could cover the price of tuition with their grant aid. In addition, officials at one public 2-year college described how their state board of education would not allow them to increase their tuition more than 5 percent each year, while officials at a public 4-year college said that any public school in their state that increased their designated tuition by a certain percentage had to set aside more money for financial aid to their students. Finally, Stafford student loan borrowing that occurred after the loan limit increases presented a mixed picture. The proportion of students taking out the maximum in Stafford student loans continued to decline between academic years 2007-08 and 2011-12 for unsubsidized (24 to 20 percent) and combined loans (61 to 58 percent) but not for subsidized loans, which increased from 54 to 57 percent in the number of students borrowing the maximum loan amount (see figure 5).

PRIVATE STUDENT LOAN BORROWING DECLINED AFTER THE LOAN LIMITS INCREASED

The landscape of private education borrowing has changed since the loan limit increases took effect. Before the loan limit increases, the total number of students borrowing private student loans had been increasing, rising by 188 percent from 961,356 to 2,764,469 students between academic years 2003-04 and 2007-08 (see Figure 6). After the loan limit increases went into effect, the number of students taking out private student loans dropped overall by 52 percent, down to 1,325,997 students between academic years 2007-08 and 2011-12. This pattern persisted across all types of institutions of higher education, with the steepest declines at public 2-year (61 percent) and for-profit 2-and 4-year institutions (58 percent) over this time period, according to Education data. While it is unclear why there were steeper declines among these types of institutions, increases in the availability of other types of aid may have been a contributing factor. For example, officials at one for-profit 4-year institution participating in our study told us they increased the amount of scholarship assistance available to students. Similarly, the financial aid administrator at a public 2-year school told us the school was able to increase institutional aid to students because its foundation aggressively sought grants to fund scholarships.

Students also borrowed less private student loan money after the loan limit increases, on average about $1,179 less in academic year 2011-12 than in academic year 2007-08– approximately a 17 percent decrease (see table 3). While the decline in the amount students borrowed occurred across all higher education institution types, amounts borrowed by students attending public 2-year schools (28 percent) and private nonprofit 4-year schools (22 percent) dropped the most. In terms of average amounts borrowed in dollars, student borrowing at private nonprofit 4-year schools showed the largest dollar decline: about $2,178. The decrease in the average private loan amount borrowed by students at public 2-year schools may have resulted in part from the effort by school officials to rein in student borrowing and the increased availability of other aid. For example, the financial aid administrator at a public 2-year school said they encourage students to pursue federal loans first and private loans as a last resort. Officials at a private nonprofit 4-year institution said they adopted an "interventionist" approach toward students who were considering private student loans. These officials said they reached out to students who were considering private student loans and, in some instances, increased the amount of institutional aid to students so that they would not need to take out private loans. Private lenders we interviewed also said that they had to rein in student borrowing to reduce the risk of loan defaults. One lender said that some lenders decreased loans to students at for-profit schools because of low graduation rates and high default rates.[22]

The decline in the number of students borrowing private student loans paralleled other declines in the private education market. According to a study by the CFPB—the agency that supervises large banks and nonbanks that make private student loans[23]—new loans for nine major lenders steadily increased from 2005, peaking in 2008 at $10.1 billion. However, in 2009, the calendar year the second loan limit increase took effect, new loans decreased 31 percent (dropping from $10.1 billion in 2008 to $7 billion in 2009). From 2009 to 2010, new loans dropped another 20 percent to $5.6 billion (See Figure 7).

As the average amount of private student loans borrowed by students dropped, the average amount of federal education loans at all institutions increased (see Figure 8). For example, between academic years 2007-08 and 2011-12, the average amount of private loans borrowed by students at public 2-year institutions dropped by 28 percent while the average amount of federal loans increased by 16 percent. At for-profit 2- and 4- year institutions, there was about an 11 percent decrease in the average amount of private student loans borrowed and a 22 percent increase in the amount of federal student loans. The trend of less reliance on private student loans and more on federal student loans to fund education persisted across all types of institutions.

Factors Contributing to Private Loan Declines

Overall, the turmoil in the nation's financial markets and the resulting recession set the stage for the declines in private loan borrowing and lending, but there were other contributing factors, too.

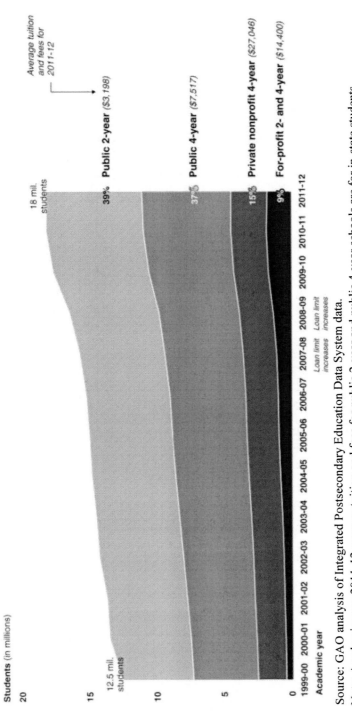

Students (in millions)

20

15 — 12.5 mil. students

10

5

0

1999-00 2000-01 2001-02 2002-03 2003-04 2004-05 2005-06 2006-07 2007-08 2008-09 2009-10 2010-11 2011-12

Academic year

18 mil. students

Average tuition and fees for 2011-12

39% **Public 2-year** *($3,198)*

37% **Public 4-year** *($7,517)*

15% **Private nonprofit 4-year** *($27,046)*

9% **For-profit 2- and 4-year** *($14,400)*

Loan limit increases

Loan limit increases

Source: GAO analysis of Integrated Postsecondary Education Data System data.

Note: Academic year 2011-12 average tuition and fees for public 2-year and public 4-year schools are for in-state students.

Figure 3. Enrollment in Degree-granting Institutions of Higher Education by Sector and Share of Students, Academic Years 1999-2000 to 2011-12 for Full- and Part-time Undergraduate Students.

Table 3. Changes in Average Private Loan Amount Borrowed by Students and Their Families by Sector, Academic Years 2003-04, 2007-08, and 2011-12

Sector	Academic year 2003-04	Academic year 2007-08	Dollar difference between academic years 2003-04 and 2007-08	Percent change between academic years 2003-04 and 2007-08	Academic year 2007-08	Academic year 2011-12	Dollar difference between academic years 2007-08 and 2011-12	Percent change between academic years 2007-08 12
Public 4- year	$6,453	$6,620	+$167	+3%	$6,620	$5,455	-$1,165	-18%
Public 2- year	4,191	3,942	-248	-6	3,942	2,828	-1,115	-28
Private nonprofit 4- year	9,303	9,899	+596	+6	9,899	7,721	-2,178	-22
For-profit 2- and 4- year	7,020	6,713	-307	-4	6,713	6,006	-707	-11
Total	7,169	7,048	-121	-2	7,048	5,870	-1,179	-17

Source: GAO analysis of National Postsecondary Student Aid Study data.

Note: Dollar difference between academic years may not be exact due to rounding.

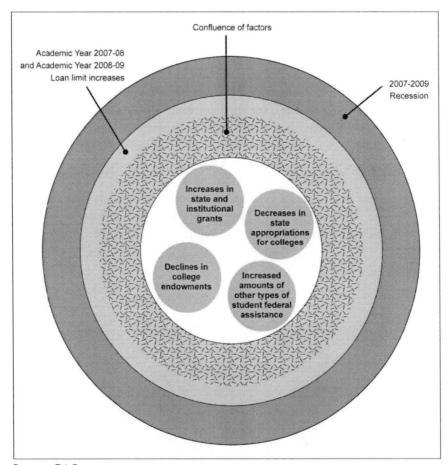

Source: GAO.

Figure 4. Confluence of Factors Occurring During Loan Limit Increases.

- **Lender exit**. In response to the turmoil in the financial markets, some lenders exited the student loan industry altogether, according to a study by CFPB. These actions changed the market from one with many lenders to a smaller market dominated by a few large lenders.
- **More stringent lending criteria**. Lenders responded to the crisis by tightening their lending criteria, making it more difficult for some students to obtain these loans, according to a study by the CFPB which was echoed by lenders and subject matter specialists we interviewed. The CFPB study found that in the years leading up to the 2007-2009 recession when private student lending was increasing,

lenders were making a higher percentage of loans to borrowers with weaker credit qualifications.[24] This trend reversed during the recession. In the aftermath of the credit crisis and recession, private lenders changed their criteria for making student loans. For example, the CFPB study found that lenders began to rely more heavily on criteria that had been traditionally used to determine a borrower's creditworthiness, such as the borrower's ability to repay the loan and individual repayment history as reflected by a borrower's Fair Isaac Corporation credit score (FICO).[25] Many lenders also required or strongly encouraged students to have a co-signer for their private student loans. While students could still obtain loans without a co-signer, lenders said student borrowers with a co-signer are more likely to secure a lower interest rate and more favorable loan terms.[26]

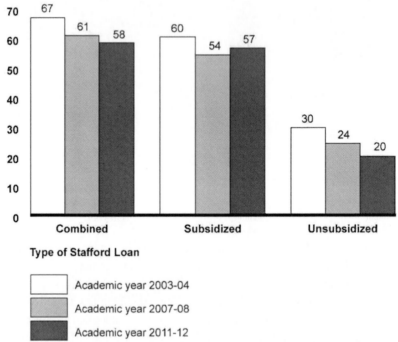

Source: GAO analysis of National Postsecondary Student Aid Study data.

Figure 5. Proportion of Eligible Students Who Borrowed at Their Maximum, Academic Years 2003-04, 2007-08, and 2011-12, by Stafford Loan Type.

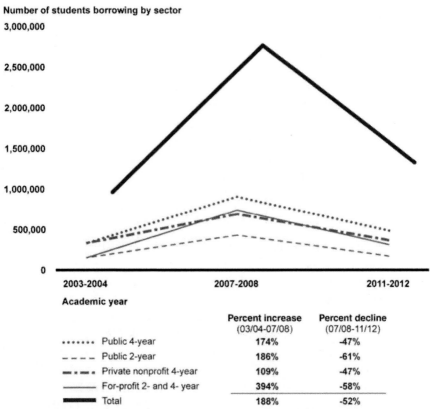

Source: GAO analysis of National Postsecondary Student Aid Study data.

Figure 6. Total Number of Students Using Private Student Loans, Academic Years 2003-04, 2007-08 and 2011-12.

- **New consumer protections**. In addition, the fallout from the turmoil in the national financial markets in 2008 increased scrutiny of the private student loan market, and subsequent statutory changes increased consumer protections (see table 4). Enacted in 2008, the Higher Education Opportunity Act (HEOA)[27] amended the Truth in Lending Act (TILA) and the Higher Education Act of 1965 to add new disclosure requirements related to private student loan rates, terms, and the availability of federal student loans. For example, it provided for a 3-day period after consummation of the loan during which a borrower may cancel a loan without penalty[28] and also provided that a borrower has 30 days after a loan is approved to accept the loan, during which time the lender generally cannot change the loan rates or terms.[29] The new disclosures were accompanied by new borrower responsibilities. In an effort to prevent over-borrowing, applicants for private student loans must now complete a self-certification form that includes a calculation of how much the student needs to borrow, and attest that they are aware of the federal loan options available to them.[30] See Appendix IV for a sample self-certification template. Several of the officials we interviewed noted that the self-certification forms helped to keep students from borrowing more funds than they actually need for educational costs. Furthermore, the HEOA amended the TILA to prohibit certain practices by private lenders, including revenue sharing between creditors and educational institutions.[31] (See table 4 for more information).

- **Proactive school initiatives.** Officials at all of the schools in our study described a wide range of activities they implemented to raise student awareness and understanding of the various types of financial aid available to them. Some school officials also described efforts aimed at providing students with alternatives to private student loans. While most of the schools provided personal counseling to help students understand the obligations that come with borrowing private student loans, financial literacy training, and a wide range of online tools to help students calculate their college costs and financial need, they also told us about efforts that were unique to their own institutions. For example, officials at one public 4-year university described how 80 to 90 percent of their students are eligible for Pell grants, which cover much of their costs, and that many students do not have the credit scores to qualify for private student loans. Officials told us that they kept tuition at a level that would enable students' Pell grants to cover the full cost of tuition. Rather than raise tuition, school officials said the school made modest increases to room and board prices for students who chose to live on campus.

  Officials at another public 4-year university said that they were able to hold tuition steady by increasing enrollment. They said that they have a multi-year plan to increase enrollment, especially for students served through their online education programs. These officials also described how they now offer a $10,000 degree to students who pursue a Bachelor's degree in the specific field of organizational leadership. The program is competency-based rather than semester credit-hour based, and features a combination of traditional classroom instruction and credit for life learning. The $10,000 cost of the degree covers tuition and fees but not room and board, transit, or other miscellaneous costs. In addition, officials at both public 4-year institutions said that their state boards of education require them to keep college prices below a certain designated threshold, and if they go above it, they must then increase the amount of institutional aid to students. Their states put this policy in place, they said, to make college more affordable and reduce the need for students to seek private student loans to finance their education.

Officials at a private nonprofit 4-year institution described an aggressive strategy for helping students pay for their education without private or federal student loans. According to these financial aid administrators, the university has adopted a policy of fully meeting each student's financial aid need and that for all students in general, they have a no loan policy. To carry out this policy, the administrators said the university does not include loans when determining a student's financial aid award and has increased institutional funding for students through grants and scholarships. According to university officials, during the recession they tapped into the university's operating funds to ensure sufficient levels of grant aid for students. In addition, they said the university has changed the way it calculates a student's financial need for purposes of institutional aid by eliminating home equity as a factor when considering a student's eligibility for institutional aid. The elimination of home equity as an asset, school officials said, resulted in more students from middle income families qualifying for financial aid.

Officials at all three for-profit institutions we interviewed said that keeping costs down is a significant part of their effort to reduce students' reliance on loans, similar to the efforts that public institutions reported. Officials at one of the for-profit institutions participating in our study said they are focusing on reducing costs for academically gifted students by increasing merit-based financial aid. Students with higher admission test scores and GPAs receive more aid than other students. The same institution also recently announced that it is offering students in its honors program full tuition for their fourth year of school. Officials at another for-profit institution told us that the number of its students using private student loans had decreased to 11 percent in 2009 and has remained at that level. School officials saw this as particularly notable because students' private loan usage had been as high as 30 percent in some years preceding 2009. School officials told us that students who are considering private student loans must participate in an interview at the school so that they fully understand the terms and conditions of their private loan. During the interview, the student is given information about private loan interest rates, and information about federal loans. School officials told us they encourage students considering loans to exhaust their federal loans before they take out private loans.

AGENCY COMMENTS AND OUR EVALUATION

We provided a draft of this report to the Department of Education and Consumer Financial Protection Bureau for review and comment. The Department of Education and the Consumer Financial Protection Bureau had no comments.

Jacqueline M. Nowicki
Acting Director
Education, Workforce, and Income Security Issues

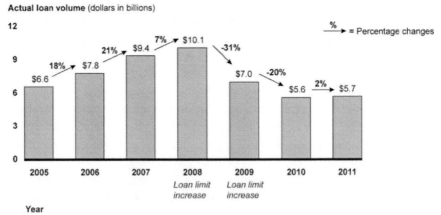

Source: GAO analysis of Consumer Financial Protection Bureau data.

Figure 7. Private Student Loan Origination Volumes before and after Federal Student Loan Limit Increases as Reported by Nine Major Lenders.

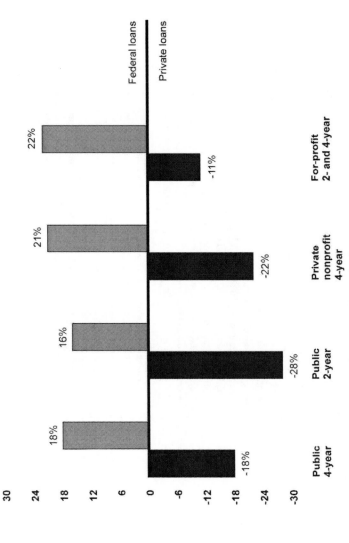

Percentage change

Federal loans

Private loans

22%
-11%
**For-profit
2- and 4-year**

21%
-22%
**Private
nonprofit
4-year**

16%
-28%
**Public
2-year**

18%
-18%
**Public
4-year**

30 24 18 12 6 0 -6 -12 -18 -24 -30

Source: GAO analysis of National Postsecondary Student Aid Study data.

Figure 8. Percentage Change in Average Amounts of Private and Federal Student Loans Borrowed Between Academic Years 2007-08 and 2011-12.

Table 4. Selected Laws and Provisions that Increased Consumer Protections

Name of law	Selected provisions

Title X of the Higher Education Opportunity Act (HEOA) (Private Student Loan Transparency and Improvement Act of 2008)	• Extends coverage of Truth in Lending Act provisions to private student loans over $25,000.[a]
	• Amends Truth in Lending Act (TILA) by requiring disclosures to borrower by private student lenders in loan applications, solicitations, approvals, and consummations, including information related to such topics as:
	  • interest rates and type of rate, such as fixed or variable
	  • interest rate adjustments, such as frequency and amount
	  • finance charges, fees, and penalties associated with default or late payment
	  • payment deferral options
	  • federal financial aid availability and applicable interest rates.
	• Borrower guaranteed 30 days after loan approval to accept rates and terms of loan as offered with no changes (except for changes based on adjustments to the index used for a loan).
	• Borrower granted 3-day right-to-cancel period.
	• Includes measures to prevent unfair and deceptive practices in private student lending:
	  • private student lenders may not:
	    • offer or provide gifts to educational institutions in exchange for any advantage related to private loan activities.
	    • engage in revenue sharing with educational institutions.
	    • use the name, emblem, mascot or logo of educational institution.
	    • impose a fee or penalty on borrower for early repayment of private student loan.

Title I, Part E of Higher Education Act of 1965, as added by section 120 of Higher Education Opportunity Act	• Among other things, requires institutions and institution-affiliated organizations that provide information regarding private student loans to:
	  • provide borrowers the private student loan disclosures required under the Truth in Lending Act.
	  • inform borrowers that they may qualify for federal student aid under Title IV and that terms and conditions of federal student loans may be more favorable than the provisions of private student loans.
	  • ensure that the information regarding private student loans is presented in a way so as to be distinct from information regarding Title IV loans.

Name of law	Selected provisions
Dodd-Frank Wall Street Reform and Consumer Protection Act[b]	Created a new federal agency—the Consumer Financial Protection Bureau (CFPB)—as an independent bureau within the Federal Reserve with the authority to supervise large banks and nonbanks that make private student loans for compliance with the federal consumer financial laws and other purposes. CFPB has authority to take enforcement action against these entities for violation of federal consumer financial laws and to take action to prevent unfair, deceptive, or abusive acts or practices in connection with a consumer financial product or service. CFPB recently issued final regulations—effective March 1, 2014—that establish its supervisory authority over any nonbank student loan servicer that handles more than one million borrower accounts.[c]

Source: GAO analysis of relevant federal laws and regulations.

Note: For purposes of these provisions, a private student loan is defined as a loan provided by a private student lender that is made expressly for postsecondary educational expenses, excluding open-end credit, real estate, secured loans, and federal loans made under Title IV of the HEA. 15 U.S.C. § 1650(a)(7).

[a] The Truth in Lending Act provides consumer protections for credit and borrowing. These protections include requirements lenders must meet when offering credit and loans to borrowers, such as disclosures about loan rates and loan terms. See 15 U.S.C. § 1601 et seq. Section 1022 of the HEOA amended TILA section 104(3), codified at 15 U.S.C. § 1603(3), to expressly cover private student loans even when the amount financed was over $25,000. At the time HEOA was enacted, certain credit transactions in which the financed amount exceeded $25,000 were exempt from TILA cost disclosure requirements. The exemption amount was raised to $50,000 in 2010 by the Dodd-Frank Wall Street Reform and Consumer Protection Act. Pub. L. No. 111-203, § 1100E(a)(1), 124 Stat. 1376, 2111 (2010).

[b] Pub. L. No. 111-203, 124 Stat. 1376 (2010).

[c] Defining Larger Participants of the Student Loan Servicing Market, 78 Fed. Reg. 73,383 (Dec. 6, 2013) (to be codified at 12 C.F.R. pt. 1090).

APPENDIX I. OBJECTIVES, SCOPE, AND METHODOLOGY

This appendix discusses our methodology for the study, which was framed around two objectives: (1) the extent, if any, that Stafford loan limit increases affected tuition, fees, and room and board prices at institutions of higher education; and (2) the trends in private student loan borrowing since the loan limits took effect.

For our first objective, we developed a panel regression model—a statistical method where data are collected over time from the same panel to explore possible relationships among events—to examine the impact of Stafford loan limit increases on tuition, fees, and room and board prices at higher education institutions. This model is described in Appendix II.[32] We conducted supplemental analyses of Department of Education (Education) data to determine patterns in college prices, enrollment, and students' use of federal student loans before and after the loan limits took effect. For this objective, we also interviewed college officials to better understand the extent to which, if any, loan limit increases influenced how they set prices, such as tuition, fees, and room and board.

For our second objective, we analyzed Education data on private student loans, reviewed results of a private student lenders survey conducted in a study by the Consumer Financial Protection Bureau (CFPB), the agency that supervises large banks and nonbanks that make private student loans.[33] We also interviewed college officials about private student loan borrowing. For both objectives, we reviewed relevant federal laws, reports, and other information relevant to these issues.

We assessed the reliability of the Education data we used by testing it for accuracy and completeness and reviewing documentation about systems used to produce the data. We found the data we reviewed reliable for the purposes of our analyses. Similarly, we assessed the reliability of the CFPB study's private student lender survey data by reviewing documentation about systems used to produce the data and reviewing the survey methodology. We conducted this performance audit from December 2012 to February 2014 in accordance with generally accepted government auditing standards. Those standards require that we plan and perform the audit to obtain sufficient, appropriate evidence to provide a reasonable basis for our findings and conclusions based on our audit objectives. We believe that the evidence we obtained provides a reasonable basis for our findings and conclusions based on our audit objectives.

Analysis of Education Data on Trends in College Prices, Enrollment, and Federal Student Loan Borrowing Patterns

To determine trends in college prices since the loan limits took effect, we examined 13 years of trend data (academic years 1999-2000 through 2011-12) for all Title IV-eligible, degree-granting institutions of higher education from Education's Integrated Postsecondary Education Data System (IPEDS), and from the three most recent National Postsecondary Student Aid Study (NPSAS) results (academic years 2003-04, 2007-08, and 2011-12). We examined this data for undergraduate students—the majority of college students—across four institutional sectors (nonprofit, for-profit, public 2-year, and public 4-year colleges) and geographic regions.[34] For public 2-year and public 4-year colleges, we also reviewed the annual tuition for both in-state and out-of-state students.[35] We analyzed three descriptors of price:

1. Tuition and fees: the amount of tuition and required fees covering a full academic year charged to students. These values represent what a typical student would be charged and may not be the same for all students at an institution. Tuition and fees data are weighted by undergraduate enrollment. We analyzed these data by sector and by region.
   Source: IPEDS and NPSAS data.

2. Total price of attendance: what a typical student would pay for tuition and required fees, books and supplies, room and board, and other personal expenses. We analyzed these data by sector.[36]
   Source: NPSAS data.

3. Net price after grants: the total price of attendance minus all grant aid received by a typical student. We analyzed these data by sector.[37]
   Source: NPSAS data.

To determine patterns in undergraduate student enrollment, we used IPEDS to analyze enrollment trends from academic years 1999-2000 through 2011-12. To determine the characteristics of enrolled students, we also analyzed IPEDS data on institutional characteristics (geographic region and sector) and student characteristics (attendance status and race and ethnicity).

To determine the extent to which students borrowed Stafford loans at their maximum levels in academic year 2011-12, we used NPSAS data. For each loan type, we analyzed and compared the proportion of eligible borrowers who received their maximum Stafford loan amount in academic years 2003-04, 2007-08, and 2011-12.

Because NPSAS data are based on probability samples, estimates are formed using the appropriate estimation weights provided with each survey's data. Because each of these samples follows a probability procedure based on random selection, they represent only one of a large number of samples that could have been drawn. Since each sample could have provided different estimates, we express our confidence in the precision of our particular sample's results as a 95 percent confidence interval (e.g., plus or minus 2.5 percentage points). This is the interval that would contain the actual population value for 95 percent of the samples we could have drawn. Unless otherwise noted, all percentage estimates from NPSAS have 95 percent confidence intervals that are within 8 percent of the estimate itself. All NPSAS dollar estimates have 95 percent confidence intervals that are within 8 percentage points of the estimate itself.

Analysis of Data on Private Student Loan Borrowing

To determine trends in private student loan borrowing since the loan limits took effect, we reviewed aggregate trend data from nine major private student lenders[38] compiled in a CFPB study from calendar years 2005-11. CFPB officials told us that the portfolios of these nine major lenders represent about 90 percent of the private student loan market. The lenders' participation in the data collection was voluntary, and the information was provided to CFPB and Education under a non-disclosure agreement and is protected under various federal laws as proprietary and confidential business information.

These private lender data consists of:

1. Sample loan-level data: records from all private student loans originated from calendar years 2005 to 2011 of nine major lenders were pooled and analyzed in the CFPB study. The data do not identify the specific lender for each loan.
2. Lender portfolio-level data: quarterly performance data on private student loans originated and/or purchased by the nine major student loan lenders who provided the loan-level data, aggregated across lenders.

In addition, the CFPB study queried the nine lenders about current loan terms and conditions. We reviewed the CFPB study, including data appendices that described these data sources and methodology. To obtain additional information about trends after the loan limit increases, we supplemented the CFPB study data with analyses of Education's IPEDS data (academic years 1999-2000 through 2011-12) and NPSAS data (academic years 1999-2000, 2007-08, and 2011-12) about private loan usage and undergraduate borrowing. We also examined these data by institutional sector and for undergraduate students only.

Interviews with College Officials, Private Student Lenders and Other Experts

To provide the schools' perspectives about the role of loan limit increases on college prices and federal and private borrowing trends, we supplemented our data analysis with interviews with college officials at eight institutions. We selected a nonprobability sample of institutions to represent each major sector of higher education and different regions, amounts of federal aid received, enrollment sizes, admission selectivity levels, and prices of tuition and related fees (see table 5). During these interviews, we spoke with the financial aid directors and other school officials with knowledge of how tuition, fees, and other prices are set, asking a series of questions related to the setting of tuition and other prices and the role of loan limit increases in setting tuition and other prices. We also asked them a series of questions about private student loans, including trends in private student borrowing among their students and the type of information they provide students to help inform their decision about whether to borrow private student loans.

We also interviewed officials for three of the largest private student lenders, who also participated in the CFPB study's lender survey. We asked them a series of questions, including questions about the trends in private student lending, how they disclose the terms of their loans and the loan certification process, how private student lending has changed over time, and whether they expected to see resurgence in the private student loan market.

In addition, we interviewed representatives from relevant professional associations, federal officials, and subject matter specialists, including academic researchers.

Table 5. Characteristics of Institutions of Higher Education Included in Our Interviews, Academic Year 2012-13

Sector	Region	Percent of Stafford loans distributed to this school's sector	Under-graduate enrollment	Total price of attendance (living on campus)	Percent of students admitted	Student demographics	Percent of beginning under-graduate students with federal loans[a]	Percent of beginning under-graduate students receiving institutional aid[a]
Public 4-year	South West	39-41%	6,868	In-state: $20,883 Out-of-state: $31,413	39%	58% White 19% Black/African American 18% Hispanic/Latino 2% Asian 1% American Indian or Alaska Native	59%	49%
Public 4-year	Great Lakes	39-41%	2,116	In-state: $17,352 Out-of-state: $24,572	37%	95% Black/African American 2% White 1% Hispanic/Latino 1% Unknown	89%	86%
Public 2-year	Rocky Mountains	7-15%	9,266	In-state: $13,658 Out-of-state: $16,738	Open admissions/all students accepted	76% White 16% Hispanic/Latino 2% Native Hawaiian or other	32%	42%

Sector	Region	Percent of Stafford loans distributed to this school's sector	Under-graduate enrollment	Total price of attendance (living on campus)	Percent of students admitted	Student demographics	Percent of beginning under-graduate students with federal loans[a]	Percent of beginning under-graduate students receiving institutional aid[a]
For-profit 2- and 4-year	New England	21%	6,546	$43,630	58%	36 Pacific Islander 2% Unknown 1% Asian 1% Black/ African American 1% American Indian or Alaska Native % White 28% Unknown 24% Black/ African American 8% Hispanic/ Latino 1% Asian 1% American Indian or Alaska Native	87%	48%
For-profit 2- and 4-year	Multiple	21%	59,484 overall	Varies	Varies	38% White 21% Black/ African American 17% Unknown	Varies	Varies

Table 5. (Continued)

Sector	Region	Percent of Stafford loans distributed to this school's sector	Under-graduate enrollment	Total price of attendance (living on campus)	Percent of students admitted	Student demographics	Percent of beginning under-graduate students with federal loans[a]	Percent of beginning under-graduate students receiving institutional aid[a]
For-profit 2- and 4-year	Multiple	21%	125,560 overall[b]	Varies	Varies	16% Hispanic/ Latino 4% Asian .6% Native Hawaiian or other Pacific Islander .6% American Indian or Alaska Native Varies	Varies	Varies
Private nonprofit 4-year	Southeast	23-33%	10,590	$58,782	40%	43% White 23% Hispanic/ Latino 7% Black/ African American 6% Unknown 5% Asian	34%	69%

Sector	Region	Percent of Stafford loans distributed to this school's sector	Under-graduate enrollment	Total price of attendance (living on campus)	Percent of students admitted	Student demographics	Percent of beginning under-graduate students with federal loans[a]	Percent of beginning under-graduate students receiving institutional aid[a]
Private nonprofit 4-year	Mid-East	23%–33%	5,327	$54,780	8%	48% White 19% Asian 7% Hispanic/ Latino 7% Black/ African American 3% Unknown	3%	60%

Source: GAO analysis of the Integrated Postsecondary Education Data System and college reports.

a Data for beginning undergraduate students receiving federal loans or institutional aid is from academic year 2011-2012.

b Enrollment data for this higher education institution is as of October 2013.

APPENDIX II. ANALYSIS OF THE RELATIONSHIP BETWEEN STUDENT LOAN LIMIT INCREASES AND TUITION

This appendix provides the methodology we used to develop a panel regression model to analyze the relationship between Stafford student loan limit increases and college prices, and the results of that analysis. Our panel regression model is a statistical method where data are collected over a series of years for the same colleges to estimate possible relationships among certain variables, controlling for the effects of other variables; in this study, the relationship was between increases in loan limits and increases in college prices.

Methodology

Our analysis of the relationship between loan limit increases and college prices used a panel regression model, which allows one to compare the same group of institutions over multiple years. Our panel dataset consists of all Title IV-eligible colleges in the United States over an 8-year time span that covers years before and after the change in loan limits, which occurred in academic years 2007-08 and 2008-09. The dataset is divided by the type of institution and the control variables used in the regression include college fixed effects, economic variables, and college characteristics. We examined the following sectors: public 4-year colleges; private nonprofit 4-year colleges; private for-profit 4-year colleges; public 2-year colleges; private for-profit 2-year colleges; and private for-profit less-than-2-year colleges. The main source of data is IPEDS, an annual survey of colleges conducted by the Department of Education (Education) that collects financial characteristics of the institutions and is maintained by Education.

Model

The base specification of our model is given by the equation:

1. CollegePrices(i,t) = B0(i) + B1*LoanLimit(t) + B2*CollegeVars(i,t)
    + B3*EconVars(t) + B4*Pre-LoanLimitTrend(t)
    + B5*Post-LoanLimitTrend(t) + e(i,t)

where the notation means the following:

- The subscript i represents college "i"
- The subscript t represents year "t"
- CollegePrices are the prices for a college in a certain year. We used undergraduate tuition and fees and price of attendance (i.e., tuition plus fees, room and board, books and supplies, and other expenses). We used in-state tuition for public institutions, out-of-state tuition for private 2- and 4-year colleges, and trade tuition for private, less-than- 2-year colleges.
- LoanLimit identifies the period following the increase in the Stafford student loan limit. The starting period for the increase in limits for both the subsidized and unsubsidized loans was academic year 2007-08 (when the limit was increased from $2,625 to $3,500 for dependent students), and academic year 2008-09 (when the loan limit was increased from $3,500 to $5,500) for unsubsidized or combined loans. We used dummy variables that are zero in the years before the change in loan limit and one in the years thereafter. The dummy variables for the loan limits in academic years 2007-08 and 2008-09 are used, respectively, in separate equations because the dummy variables overlap. The loan limit increases are one-time events. In addition to the loan limit increases, these variables also capture the effects on college prices of other events that occurred at the same time, such as the onset of the 2007-2009 financial crises and recession.
- B0 is a college fixed effect. The fixed effect allows us to control for characteristics of the college, which do not vary over time and may affect the college prices, but are not observed in our data. For example, the college may be located in an expensive region of the country.
- CollegeVars are variables that describe characteristics of a college in a certain year. The key variables we used involve revenue, and include state appropriations and endowment income. We also included the number of undergraduates (in full-time equivalents).
- EconVars are control variables that vary by year, but not by college. These variables reflect general economic conditions and include state-level unemployment, housing prices, and a stock market index.

- Pre-LoanLimitTrend and Post-LoanLimitTrend: To capture trends in college prices during the periods before and after the loan limit increases, two different time trends were used. For regressions analyzing the effect of the academic year 2007-08 loan limit increase on college prices:

2. Pre-LoanLimitTrend = $(t - 2008)*(1 - \text{LoanLimit})$, and
3. Post-LoanLimitTrend = $(t - 2008 + 1)*\text{LoanLimit}$.

In Equations (2) and (3), 2008 will be replaced with 2009 for regressions analyzing the effect of the academic year 2008-09 loan limit increase on college prices. The post-loan limit trend is implicitly an interaction term between the loan limit variable and a time trend.

These variables control for trends in college prices that are common to all colleges in our sample. Including both variables in our regressions allows trends in college prices after the loan limit increase to differ from trends in college prices before the loan limit increase. However, these variables also reflect changes in other unobservable factors, such as economic or political conditions, that may cause trends in college prices to differ before and after the loan limit increases.

- e is the error term, which captures potential model misspecification, measurement errors, and unobserved variables.

We divided the sample into sectors based on the control (e.g. public, private, and nonprofit, for profit) and level (e.g. 2-year, 4-year) of the institution. Specifically, we examined the six sectors where there were sufficient observations for meaningful analysis and excluded the remaining three sectors because there were too few observations. Thus we included public 4-year colleges; private nonprofit 4-year colleges; private for-profit 4-year colleges; public 2-year colleges; private for-profit 2-year colleges; and private for-profit less-than-2-year colleges and excluded private nonprofit less than two-year colleges.

The analysis was done separately by institutional sector for two reasons. First, different institution types may not necessarily compete for the same types of students. For example, students with lower household incomes are less likely to attend private colleges than public colleges. Thus, different sectors may use different strategies for the college prices they charge. Second, different institution types are likely to be affected by different variables. For example, state appropriations are likely to be more important to public colleges than for-profit private colleges. This implies that the model specification could be different for different sectors.

Data

The main source of data is the IPEDS dataset, maintained by Education. IPEDS is an annual survey of colleges conducted by Education which focuses on financial characteristics of the institutions. We merged the academic year data across years and colleges to form a panel that runs from the 2003-04 to the 2010-11 academic year. For certain income variables, we used definitions based on work by the Delta Cost Project. Now part of the American Institutes for Research, the Delta Cost Project published a data map with the goal of standardizing and simplifying some of the variables within IPEDS. Both IPEDS and the Delta Cost Project definitions have been used in prior GAO work and deemed reliable for our purposes.

We further refined our IPEDS data by excluding certain colleges for various reasons. The major exclusion was institutions that did not have complete data for all 8 years that we examined. Further, responding to the IPEDS survey is required only for colleges that participate in the Title IV aid programs. We also excluded colleges that were outside the 50 states and the District of Columbia, did not participate in Title IV, were not open to the public, or were not predominantly postsecondary. We also excluded colleges that were not active, were primarily administrative units, or did not have undergraduate programs. This resulted in approximately 600 public 4-year colleges; 1200 private nonprofit 4-year colleges; 400 private for-profit 4-year colleges; 1000 public 2-year colleges; 400 private for-profit 2-year colleges; and 900 private for-profit less-than-2-year colleges.[39]

We also added data from outside IPEDS to control for the potential impact of household wealth on college prices. Specifically, we added a state-level unemployment rate from the Bureau of Labor Statistics. In some versions, we added the Case-Schiller composite housing price index, which came from Standard and Poor's (S&P), and the S&P 500 stock index, which we got from Federal Reserve Economic Data (FRED) of the Federal Reserve Bank of St. Louis.

Results

We ran several versions of our model, the results of which are presented in tables 6 and 7. Table 6 shows results for the first loan limit increase in academic year 2007-08, and table 7 shows results for the second loan limit increase in academic year 2008-09—both best represent the various models we estimated. Overall, the estimated models are statistically significant as indicated by the models' statistics (p-values).

Table 6 shows the results for the academic year 2007-08 Stafford loan limit increase for both subsidized and unsubsidized loans on tuition and fees (college prices). In each estimated model, the average academic year change in college prices for years prior to the loan limit increase is given by B4 (the coefficient on Pre-LoanLimitTrend); the average academic year change in college prices in the year in which the loan limits increased relative to the prior year is given by the sum of B1 (the coefficient on LoanLimit), B4, and B5 (the coefficient on Post- LoanLimitTrend); and the average academic year change in college prices in years after the loan limit increase is given by B5, all else being equal. Thus, in the year the loan limit increases, the change in college prices resulting from the loan limit and the trend effects is the sum of B1 and B5; we could not obtain the effects of the loan limit by itself because B5 captures that effect as well as the trend effects. As shown in table 7, for example, for private, nonprofit 4-year colleges (B1 = – $698, B4 = $661, and B5 = $683), the average academic year change in college prices for years prior to the academic year 2007-08 loan limit increase is $661, the average change in college prices in the 2007-08 academic year compared to the prior year is $646, the average academic year change in college prices in years following the academic year 2007-08 loan limit increase is $683, and the average academic year change in college prices related to the loan limit increase is - $15 in the 2007-08 academic year. Estimates from the regressions analyzing the academic year 2008-09 Stafford loan limit increases for only unsubsidized loans are shown in table 8.[40]

Table 7 presents the average academic year changes in college prices by different institutions in the periods before the academic year 2007-08 Stafford loan limit increase, the changes in college prices between the loan limit year and the prior year, the change college prices in the years after the loan limit increase, and the change in college prices in the loan limit year attributable to only the events that occurred in that academic year. The results show that average academic year college prices generally increased across all types of colleges before the increase in the Stafford loan limits. In the academic year of the 2007-08 Stafford loan limit increase, college prices increased for some colleges and decreased for others. The decrease in college prices by some colleges is consistent with the opinion that the rapid change in economic conditions may have led state legislatures to put political pressure on colleges in their states to keep tuition low, a sentiment that was echoed in some of our interviews with college officials. Furthermore, some of the college officials we spoke with said that they held down tuition increases because of the economic downturn and financial crises. In the years following the academic year 2007-08 loan limit increase, college prices generally increased. Although the results appear to suggest that the loan limit increase tended to weaken the rising trend in college prices, we cannot determine which portion of the change in college prices in the academic year of the 2007-08 loan limit increase is attributable to the loan limit alone because it is confounded by other events in that year as well as the ongoing rising prices.

The results in table 9 show the average academic year changes in college prices before, during, and after the academic year 2008-09 Stafford loan limit increases. There were generally increases in college prices in the academic year of the 2008-09 loan limit increase, before and afterwards (although there were few cases of decreases). Similar to the academic year 2007-08 loan limit increase, while the results seem to suggest that the loan limit increase in academic year 2008-09 tended to boost the rising trend in college prices we could not determine the portion of the increase due solely to the loan limit increase because of other confounding effects. Also, we could not separate out the effects of the academic year 2007-08 and 2008-09 Stafford loan limit increases from each other after they occurred since the two events overlapped.

Our results suggest that average academic year college prices generally increased across all types of colleges prior to the increases in the Stafford loan limits in academic years 2007-08 and 2008-09, and after the loan limit increases. In the academic year of the 2007-08 Stafford loan limit increase college prices increased for some colleges while they decreased for others. And in the academic year of the 2008-09 Stafford loan limit increase, college prices generally increased. But, in the effective years of the loan limit increases we could not identify the changes in college prices that were due solely to the increases in the Stafford loan limit increases because of other events that happened during that time, including the financial crisis and the economic recession, as well as the upward trend in college prices.

Table 6. Regression Estimates of the Academic Year 2007-08 Stafford Loan Limit Increases and College Tuition and Fees

Sector	Public, 4-year	Private, nonprofit, 4-year	Private, for-profit, 4-year	Public, 2-year	Private, for-profit, 2-year	Private, for-profit, <2 yr
Dependent variable	In-state tuition	Out-of-state tuition	Out-of-state tuition	In-state tuition	Out-of-state tuition	Trade tuition
Loan limit dummy	-95.80 [0.19]	-698.44 [0.00]	-415.42 [0.32]	-288.63 [0.00]	-1,174.65 [0.03]	-318.78 [0.07]
Pre-loan limit trend[a]	119.53 [0.00]	660.53 [0.00]	446.75 [0.00]	81.37 [0.00]	566.53 [0.00]	325.79 [0.00]
Post-loan limit trend[b]	278.99 [0.00]	682.73 [0.00]	-49.77 [0.72]	178.74 [0.00]	30.84 [0.86]	548.98 [0.00]
State appropriations	-0.008 [0.021]	NA	NA	0.000 [0.234]	NA	NA
Endowment income	NA	-0.0005 [0.11]	NA	NA	NA	NA
State unemployment rate	82.13 [0.00]	21.53 [0.20]	-48.13 [0.42]	-50.12 [0.00]	14.48 [0.00]	97.15 [0.00]
Stock market price index	0.28 [0.05]	-0.152 [0.46]	-1.46 [0.08]	-0.363 [0.00]	- 2.14 [0.04]	0.29 [0.39]
House price index	5.59 [0.00]	-5.65 [0.01]	-1.95 [0.82]	0.342 [0.70]	6.34 [0.53] -	3.70 [0.27]
Full-time undergraduates	-0.004 [0.73]	-0.046 [0.12]	-0.027 [0.00]	0.0003 [0.95]	- 0.300 [0.12]	-0.000 [0.99]
Constant	3,908 [0.00]	21,880 [0.00]	18,188 [0.00]	3,689 [0.00]	18,029 [0.00]	9,738 [0.00]
College fixed-effects	Yes	Yes	Yes	Yes	Yes	Yes
No. of observations	4,564	9,261	2,679	7,264	2,155	6,333
No. of colleges	601	1,191	398	946	385	906
Prob > F	0.00	0.00	0.00	0.00	0.00	0.00
Adjusted R-square	0.94	0.98	0.72	0.93	0.71	0.86

Source: GAO analysis of Integrated Postsecondary Education Data System data.

Notes: The values in square brackets are the p-values of the estimates.

NA means not applicable.
a The pre-loan limit time trend is equal to 0 in 2007-08 and later, equal to -1 in 2006-07, equal to -2 in 2005-06, and so forth.
b The post-loan limit time trend is equal to 0 in 2006-07 and earlier, equal to 1 in 2007-08, equal to 2 in 2008-09, and so forth.

Table 7. Estimated Average Academic Year Changes in Tuition and Fees: Academic Year 2007-08 Stafford Loan Limit Increase

Sector	Academic Year 2007-2008 Stafford Loan Limit Increase			
	Average academic year change in tuition & fees, pre-loan limit years (2003-04 to 2006-07)[b]	Average academic year change in tuition & fees, loan limit year (2007-08)[c]	Average academic-year change in tuition & fees, loan limit year (2008-09 to 2010-11)[d]	Average academic-year change in tuition & fees from loan limit loan limit year (2007-08)[e]
Public, 4-year	$120	$303	$279	$183
Private, nonprofit, 4-year	661	646	683	-15
Private, for-profit, 4-year	447	18 -	-50	-465
Public, 2-year	81	29 -	179	-110
Private, for-profit, 2-year	567	577 -	31	-1,144
Private, for-profit, <2 -year	326	556	549	230

Source: GAO analysis of Integrated Postsecondary Education Data System data.

a The estimates are based on the coefficient estimates in Table 1.

b The value equals the pre-loan-trend in Table 1.

c The value equals the sum of loan limit dummy, pre-loan trend, and post-loan limit trend in Table 1.

d The value equals the post-loan limit trend in Table 1.

e The value equals the sum of loan limit dummy and post-loan limit trend in Table 1.

Table 8. Regression Estimates of the Academic Year 2008-09 Stafford Loan Limit Increases and College Tuition and Fees

Sector	Public, 4-year	Private, nonprofit, 4-year	Private, for-profit, 4-year	Public, 2-year	Private, for-profit, 2-year	Private, for-profit, <2-yr
Dependent variable	In-state tuition	Out-of-state tuition	Out-of-state tuition	In-state tuition	Out-of-state tuition	Trade tuition
Loan limit dummy	403.37 [0.00] -	-575.75 [0.00]	9.84 [0.98]	92.29 [0.07]	761.33 [0.19]	-590.72 [0.00]
Pre-loan limit trend[a]	183.62 [0.00]	653.03 [0.00]	293.63 [0.00]	42.91 [0.00]	183.90 [0.01]	402.69 [0.00]
Post-loan limit trend[b]	342.14 [0.00]	658.57 [0.00]	-125.43 [0.53]	139.80 [0.00]	-224.95 [0.36]	599.64 [0.00]
State appropriations	0.008 [0.02] -	NA	NA	0.000 [0.24]	NA	NA
Endowment income	NA	-0.0005 [0.11]	NA	NA	NA	NA
State unemployment rate	84.90 [0.00]	17.72 [0.30]	-42.84 [0.48]	-51.94 [0.00]	20.92 [0.82]	96.15 [0.00]
Stock market price index	0.116 [0.50] -	-0.043 [0.86]	-0.813 [0.43]	-0.123 [0.25]	-0.258 [0.83]	-0.085 [0.83]
House price index	4.51 [0.00]	-5.84 [0.00]	2.02 [0.78]	0.97 [0.20]	2.34 [0.78]	1.96 [0.50]
Full-time undergraduates	-0.004 [0.69]	-0.046 [0.12]	-0.027 [0.00]	0.000 [0.96]	-0.306 [0.11]	-0.000 [0.99]
Constant	4,943 [0.00]	22,429 [0.00]	16,512 [0.00]	3,222 [0.00]	13,205 [0.00]	11,144 [0.00]
College fixed effects	Yes	Yes	Yes	Yes	Yes	Yes
No. of observations	4,564	9,261	2,679	7,264	2,155	6,333
No. of colleges	601	1,191	398	946	385	906
Prob > F	0.00	0.00	0.00	0.00	0.00	0.00
Adjusted R-square	0.94	0.98	0.72	0.93	0.71	0.86

Source: GAO analysis of Integrated Postsecondary Education Data System data.

Notes: The values in square brackets are the p-values of the estimates.

NA means not applicable.

[a] The pre-loan limit time trend is equal to 0 in 2008-09 and later, equal to -1 in 2007-08, equal to -2 in 2006-07, and so forth.

[b] The post-loan limit time trend is equal to 0 in 2007-08 and earlier, equal to 1 in 2008-09, equal to 2 in 2009-10, and so forth.

Table 9. Estimated Average Academic Year Changes in Tuition and Fees: Academic Year 2008-09 Stafford Loan Limit

Sector	Academic year 2008-09 Stafford Loan limit increase[a]			
	Average academic year change in tuition & fees, pre-loan limit years (2003-04 to 2007-08)[b]	Average academic year change in tuition & fees, loan limit year (2008-09)[c]	Average academic year change in tuition & fees, loan-limit year (2009-10 to 2010-11)[d]	Average academic year change in tuition & fees from loan limit, loan limit year (2008-09)[e]
Public 4-year	$184	$123	$342	-61
Private nonprofit 4 year	653	736	659	83
Private for-profit 4-year	294	179	-125	-115
Public 2 year	43	275	140	232
Private for-profit 2-year	184	720	-225	536
Private for-profit <2-year	403	412	600	9

Source: GAO analysis of Integrated Postsecondary Education Data System data.

[a] The estimates are based on the coefficient estimates in Table 8.

[b] The value equals the pre-loan-trend in Table 8.

[c] The value equals the sum of loan limit dummy, pre-loan trend, and post-loan limit trend in Table 8.

[d] The value equals the post-loan limit trend in Table 8.

[e] The value equals the sum of loan limit dummy and post-loan limit trend in Table 8.

We took multiple steps to verify our methodology. First, we consulted with GAO experts on statistics, econometric modeling, and higher education issues. Based on their comments, we made modifications to our model where appropriate. Second, we consulted academic literature on student financial aid and tuition. Third, we consulted academic experts who reviewed our methodology and offered feedback. Fourth, we recognize that our analysis has some limitations, including the difficulty in isolating the effects of the Stafford loan limits themselves, the relatively small number of years used, and our inability to include other types of colleges. The results should therefore be interpreted with caution.

APPENDIX III. ADDITIONAL DATA ON COLLEGE PRICES AND STUDENT ENROLLMENT

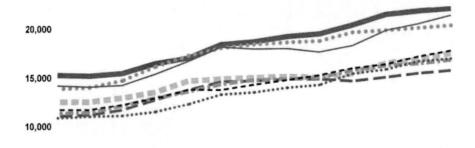

Out of state tuition and fees by region (in Academic Year 2011-12 constant dollars)

Academic year

	Region	Average annual rate increase (Academic Year 2007-08 through Academic Year 2011-12)
	New England	3%
	Middle East	4%
	Great Lakes	1%
	Plains	2%
	Southeast	2%
	Southwest	3%
	Rocky Mountains	4%
	Far West	5%

Source: GAO analysis of Integrated Postsecondary Education Data System data.

Figure 9. In-state Tuition and Required Fees by Region for Full-time Undergraduate Students, Academic Years 1999-2000 to 2011-12.

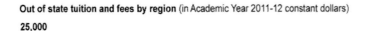

		Average annual rate increase (Academic Year 2007-08 through Academic Year 2011-12)
	New England	3%
	Middle East	4%
	Great Lakes	1%
	Plains	2%
	Southeast	2%
	Southwest	3%
	Rocky Mountains	4%
	Far West	5%

Source: GAO analysis of Integrated Postsecondary Education Data System data.

Figure 10. Out-of-state Tuition and Required Fees by Region for Full-time Undergraduate Students, Academic Years 1999-2000 to 2011-12.

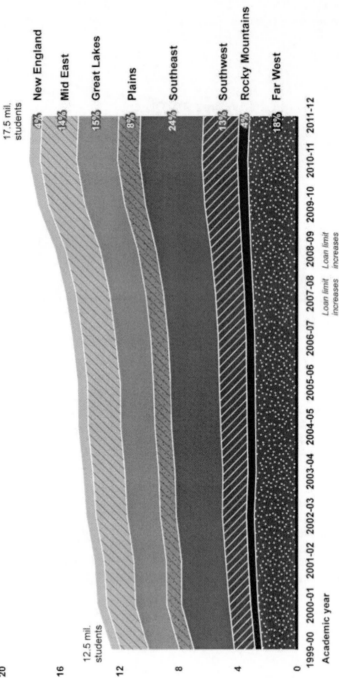

Students (in millions)

20

16

12.5 mil.
students

12

8

4

0

Academic year

1999-00 2000-01 2001-02 2002-03 2003-04 2004-05 2005-06 2006-07 2007-08 2008-09 2009-10 2010-11 2011-12

17.5 mil.
students

Loan limit
increases

Loan limit
increases

7% New England

11% Mid East

15% Great Lakes

8% Plains

24% Southeast

13% Southwest

4% Rocky Mountains

18% Far West

Source: GAO analysis of Integrated Postsecondary Education Data System data.

Figure 11. Enrollment in Degree-granting Institutions of Higher Education by Region and Share of Students, Academic Years 1999-2000 to 2011-12.

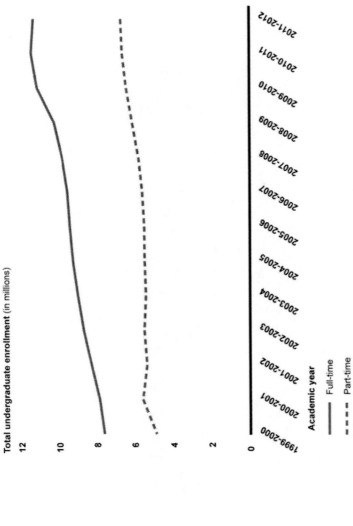

Source: GAO analysis of Integrated Postsecondary Education Data System data.

Figure 12. Enrollment in Degree-granting Institutions of Higher Education by Attendance Status, Academic Years 1999-2000 to 2011-12

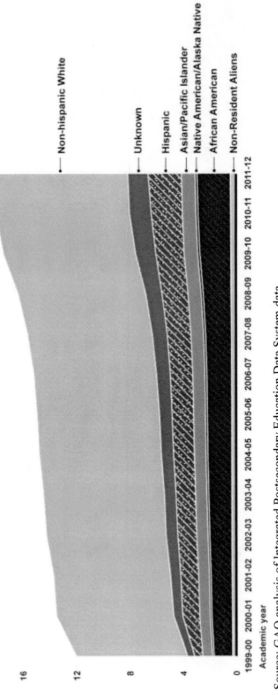

Total undergraduate enrollment by ethnicity (in millions)

Academic year

Non-hispanic White

Unknown
Hispanic
Asian/Pacific Islander
Native American/Alaska Native
African American
Non-Resident Aliens

Source: GAO analysis of Integrated Postsecondary Education Data System data.

Figure 13. Enrollment in Degree-granting Institutions of Higher Education by Ethnicity, Academic Years 1999-2000 to 2011-12.

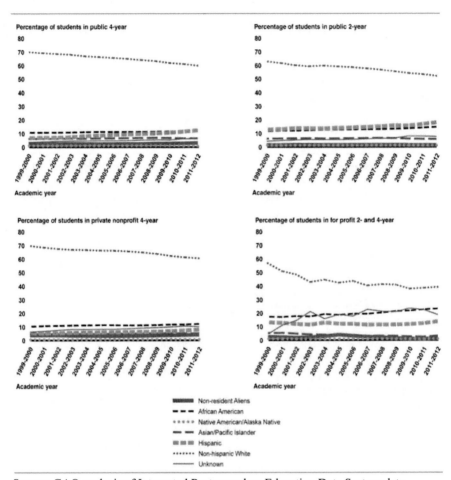

Source: GAO analysis of Integrated Postsecondary Education Data System data.

Figure 14. Enrollment in Degree-granting Institutions of Higher Education by Sector and Ethnicity, Academic Years 1999-2000 to 2011-12.

APPENDIX IV: SAMPLE SELF-CERTIFICATION FORM FOR PRIVATE LOAN APPLICANT

 **Private Education Loan
Applicant Self-Certification**

This space for lender use only

OMB No. 1845-0101
Form Approved
Exp. Date 05-31-2018

Important: Pursuant to Section 155 of the Higher Education Act of 1965, as amended, (HEA) and to satisfy the requirements of Section 128(e)(3) of the Truth in Lending Act, a lender must obtain a self-certification signed by the applicant before disbursing a private education loan. The school is required on request to provide this form or the required information only for students admitted or enrolled at the school. Throughout this Applicant Self-Certification, "you" and "your" refer to the applicant who is applying for the loan. The applicant and the student may be the same person.

Instructions: Before signing, carefully read the entire form, including the definitions and other information on the following page. Submit the signed form to your lender.

SECTION 1: NOTICES TO APPLICANT

- Free or lower-cost Title IV federal, state, or school student financial aid may be available in place of, or in addition to, a private education loan. To apply for Title IV federal grants, loans and work-study, submit a Free Application for Federal Student Aid (FAFSA) available at www.fafsa.ed.gov, or by calling 1-800-4-FED-AID, or from the school's financial aid office.
- A private education loan may reduce eligibility for free or lower-cost federal, state, or school student financial aid.
- You are <u>strongly</u> encouraged to pursue the availability of free or lower-cost financial aid with the school's financial aid office.
- The financial information required to complete this form can be obtained from the school's financial aid office. If the lender has provided this information, you should contact your school's financial aid office to verify this information and to discuss your financing options.

SECTION 2: COST OF ATTENDANCE AND ESTIMATED FINANCIAL ASSISTANCE

If information is not already entered below, obtain the needed information from the school's financial aid office and enter it on the appropriate line. Sign and date where indicated. See Section 5 for definitions of financial aid terms.

A. Student's cost of attendance for the period of enrollment covered by the loan $_____

B. Estimated financial assistance for the period of enrollment covered by the loan $_____

C. Difference between amounts A and B $_____

   WARNING: If you borrow more than the amount on line C, you risk reducing your eligibility for free or lower-cost federal, state, or school financial aid.

SECTION 3: APPLICANT INFORMATION

Enter or correct the information below.

Full Name and Address of School _____

Applicant Name (last, first, MI) _____   Date of Birth (mm/dd/yyyy)____ / ___ / _____

Permanent Street Address _____

City, State, Zip Code _____

Area Code / Telephone Number   Home (   ) _____   Other (   ) _____

E-mail Address_____

Period of Enrollment Covered by the Loan (mm/dd/yyyy)   From ____ / ____ / _____ to ____ / ____ / _____

If the student is <u>not</u> the applicant, provide the student's name and date of birth.

Student Name (last, first, MI) _____   Student Date of Birth (mm/dd/yyyy)____ / ___ / ___

SECTION 4: APPLICANT SIGNATURE

I certify that I have read and understood the notices in Section 1 and, that to the best of my knowledge, the information provided on this form is true and correct.

Signature of Applicant _____   Date (mm/dd/yyyy) _____

Source: Department of Education

End Notes

[1] Pub. L. No. 110-227, § 9, 122 Stat. 740, 748.

[2] Because data were not yet available to respond to the mandate, GAO first reported in 2009 with a briefing to Congress. The second report, *Federal Student Loans: Patterns in Tuition, Enrollment, and Federal Stafford Loan Borrowing Up to the 2007-08 Loan Limit Increase,* GAO 11-470R (Washington, D.C.: May 25, 2011), provided descriptive information on the first of the two loan limit increases, including that there was a decline in the proportion of eligible Stafford loan borrowers who borrowed their maximum under the new loan limit increase. The first loan limit increase covered fewer students, and data were not available on the second loan limit increase at the time of that report.

[3] For our panel regression model, we compared the same cohort or group of institutions over multiple years. Our panel consisted of all Title IV-eligible colleges in the United States over an 8-year time span that covered years before and after the change in loan limits, which occurred in academic years 2007-08 and 2008-09. The dataset is divided by the type of institution and the control variables used in the regression include college fixed effects, economic variables and college characteristics. For more information about our panel regression model, see Appendix II.

[4] Programs authorized under Title IV of the Higher Education Act of 1965, as amended, provide grants, loans and work-study funds from the federal government to eligible students. To receive Title IV assistance students must be enrolled in institutions of higher education that are authorized to operate in the state in which they are located, accredited by an agency recognized by the Department of Education and certified by the Department as eligible to participate in Title IV programs. An institution that enters into a program participation agreement with the Department is allowed to participate in any of the Title IV federal student financial assistance programs (other than the Leveraging Educational Assistance Partnership (LEAP) and the National Early Intervention Scholarship and Partnership (NEISP) programs).

[5] The term "nonprofit" refers to not-for-profit private colleges. Private colleges can also be for-profit, so we are making the distinction between the two by using the terms "nonprofit" and "for-profit" in this report.

[6] Our scope includes institutions of higher education in all 50 states and the District of Columbia. We grouped 2- and 4-year for-profit institutions together because about half of the institutions that classify themselves as 4-year institutions award mainly 2-year degrees. Because we defined our population of institutions of higher education as degree- granting, our analysis excludes less-than-2-year for-profit institutions that award certificates.

[7] Congress first passed a law that raised Stafford loan limits for first-and second-year undergraduate students as well as for graduate and professional students in academic year 2007-08, and subsequently for all qualified undergraduate students receiving unsubsidized Stafford loans in academic year 2008-09.

[8] Consumer Financial Protection Bureau and Department of Education, *Private Student Loans* (Washington, D.C.: August 29, 2012). For the purposes of this report, when we refer to the 'CFPB study' we mean this report that was conducted by CFPB and Education.

[9] Pub. L. No. 111-152, § 2201, 124 Stat. 1029, 1074.

[10] Congressional Budget Office, *Cost Estimate, H.R. 3221 Student Aid and Fiscal Responsibility Act of 2009* (Washington, D.C.: July 24, 2009).

[11] Postsecondary students include both graduate and undergraduate students.

[12] Regardless of loan type, borrowers must be either U.S. citizens or eligible noncitizens, and be enrolled at least half time in a degree or certificate program, among other requirements. 20 U.S.C. § 1091.

[13] 20 U.S.C. § 1087kk. The EFC represents the amount the applicant and the applicant's family can reasonably be expected to contribute toward the applicant's postsecondary education.

20 U.S.C. § 1087mm. When we use the phrase "total price of attendance" in the context of the legal requirements for the Stafford Loan program, we use it to refer to "cost of attendance" as that phrase is defined in 20 U.S.C. § 1087ll.

[14] Pub. L. No. 109-171, § 8005, 120 Stat. 4, 158 (2006). As we reported in 2011, these increases were the first changes to the Stafford loan limits since academic year 1993-94. For undergraduate students, these reflect an increase of $875 or $1,000, with the limits after the increase ranging from $3,500 to $8,500 depending on a student's class level, dependency status, and whether the student was receiving a subsidized or an unsubsidized loan.

[15] Pub. L. No. 110-227, § 2, 122 Stat. 740.

[16] For more information about our panel regression model and analysis of the relationship between Stafford loan limit increases and tuition, fees, and room and board, see Appendix II.

[17] We used three descriptors to study postsecondary prices: tuition and required fees, total price of attendance, and net price after grants. Total price of attendance is what a typical student would pay for tuition and required fees, books and supplies, room and board, and other personal expenses, and net price after grants is the total price of attendance minus all grant aid received by a typical student.

[18] While it is unclear why there was a decrease in for-profit institution tuition and fees, officials at all three of the for-profit institutions we interviewed told us that over the past few years they had decided not to raise their tuition and fees, and that they based these decisions on how their prices compared to other institutions and general affordability for students.

[19] This high percentage change in the Far West region was largely driven by changes in tuition and fees at California's institutions of higher education; California had an 18 percent increase in tuition and fees from academic years 2007-08 through 2011-12. According to a report by California's Legislative Analyst's Office, volatility in California state funding support led institutions of higher education to tap into funding reserves and take actions to reduce per student costs, such as increasing class size, furloughing employees, and reducing various campus services and overhead. See California Legislative Analyst's Office, *The 2011-12 Budget: Higher Education Budget in Context* (January 19, 2011).

[20] IPEDS includes these states in the following regions: the New England region includes Connecticut, Maine, Massachusetts, New Hampshire, Rhode Island, and Vermont; the Mid East region includes Delaware, the District of Columbia, Maryland, New Jersey, New York, and Pennsylvania; the Great Lakes region includes Illinois, Indiana, Michigan, Ohio, and Wisconsin; the Plains region includes Iowa, Kansas, Minnesota, Missouri, Nebraska, North Dakota, and South Dakota; the Southeast region includes Alabama, Arkansas, Florida, Georgia, Kentucky, Louisiana, Mississippi, North Carolina, South Carolina, Tennessee, Virginia, and West Virginia; the Southwest region includes Arizona, New Mexico, Oklahoma, and Texas; the Rocky Mountains region includes Colorado, Idaho, Montana, Utah, and Wyoming; and the Far West region includes Alaska, California, Hawaii, Nevada, Oregon, and Washington.

[21] The most recent data available cites this figure for the period spanning years 2001 through 2011. See U.S. Department of Education, National Center for Education Statistics, *Digest of Education Statistics, 2012*, NCES 2014-015, Chapter 3.

[22] A CFPB and Education report also showed that students at for-profit colleges have lower completion and graduation rates and higher rates of default on private student loans than students attending other types of institutions. For more information, see Consumer Financial Protection Bureau and Department of Education, *Private Student Loans* (Washington, D.C.: August 29, 2012).

[23] The CFPB study collected information about all loan originations between calendar years 2005 and 2011 from a sample of nine major lenders who were active in the industry in 2012. The estimated 2011 market size when including other lenders not included in the sample was $7 billion (origination volume) and $150 billion (outstanding volume) (compared to $140.2

billion outstanding for sample lenders). See Consumer Financial Protection Bureau and Department of Education, *Private Student Loans* (Washington, D.C.: 2012).

[24] See CFPB and Education, *Private Student Loans.*

[25] The Fair Isaac Corporation credit score, generally referred to as a FICO score, is a score that many lenders use to determine the creditworthiness of loan applicants. The score is calculated from a borrower's payment history, including late and missed payments, length of credit history, type of credit used by the borrower, such as installment loans, and other factors.

[26] See CFPB and Education, *Private Student Loans.*

[27] Pub. L. No. 110-315, 122 Stat. 3078 (2008).

[28] *Id.*, at § 1021(a), 122 Stat. 3483, codified at 15 U.S.C. § 1638(e)(7).

[29] *Id.*, at § 1021(a), 122 Stat. 3483, codified at 15 U.S.C. § 1638(e)(6).

[30] *Id.*. at § 1021(a), 122 Stat. 3483, codified at 15 U.S.C. § 1638(e)(3).

[31] *Id.*, at § 1011, 122 Stat. 3479, codified at 15 U.S.C. § 1650.

[32] For our panel regression model, we compared the same group of institutions over multiple years. Our panel consisted of all Title IV-eligible colleges in the United States over an 8-year time span that covered years before and after the change in loan limits, which occurred in academic years 2007-08 and 2008-09. The dataset is divided by the type of institution, and the control variables used in the regression include college fixed effects, economic variables and college characteristics.

[33] Consumer Financial Protection Bureau and the Department of Education, *Private Student Loans* (Washington, D.C.: August 29, 2012). The survey included information from nine major lenders. The participating lenders for this CFPB and Education study included: RBS Citizens N.A., Discover Financial Services, The First Marblehead Corporation, JPMorgan Chase Bank, N.A., PNC Bank, N.A., Sallie Mae, Inc., SunTrust Banks, Inc., U.S. Bank National Association, and Wells Fargo Bank, N.A. The information was provided to Education and CFPB under a non-disclosure agreement and is protected under various federal laws as proprietary and confidential business information.

[34] Our scope includes all 50 states and the District of Columbia. We grouped 2- and 4-year for-profit institutions together because about half of the institutions that classify themselves as 4-year institutions award mainly 2-year degrees. Given that we defined our population of institutions of higher education as degree-granting, our analysis excludes less-than-2-year for-profit institutions that award certificates.

[35] We did not break down in-district and out-of-district tuition data for public 2-year institutions. Most schools that offer programs for 2 years likely do not enroll many out-of- district commuters, so the population is expected to be too small to yield reliable results.

[36] We did not analyze NPSAS data by region.

[37] We did not analyze NPSAS data by region.

[38] Consumer Financial Protection Bureau and the Department of Education, *Private Student Loans* (Washington, D.C.: August 29, 2012). The participating lenders for this study included: RBS Citizens N.A., Discover Financial Services, The First Marblehead Corporation, JPMorgan Chase Bank, N.A., PNC Bank, N.A., Sallie Mae, Inc., SunTrust Banks, Inc., U.S. Bank National Association, and Wells Fargo Bank, N.A.

[39] The exact number of observations used per sector varies by year depending on exactly which variables are used in the model. If a college has a missing value for a particular variable in a particular year, then the number of observations used in that year decreases.

[40] Our analysis of college prices based on cost of attendance, for the limited number of colleges that had enough data, are similar to the reported results for tuition and fees.

In: Students and Stafford Loans   ISBN: 978-1-63321-126-1
Editor: Daphne Rollins   © 2014 Nova Science Publishers, Inc.

Chapter 2

FEDERAL STUDENT LOANS: PATTERNS IN TUITION, ENROLLMENT, AND FEDERAL STAFFORD LOAN BORROWING UP TO THE 2007-08 LOAN LIMIT INCREASE[*]

United States Government Accountability Office

May 25, 2011
Congressional Committees
Subject: *Federal Student Loans: Patterns in Tuition, Enrollment, and Federal Stafford Loan Borrowing Up to the 2007-08 Loan Limit Increase*

Although a postsecondary education is vitally important to many individuals and the nation's ability to compete globally, high college tuition rates are prompting concerns that it may remain an elusive goal for some. To help students finance their education, Congress recently raised the ceiling on the amount individual students can borrow under the federal Stafford Loan program (referred to in legislation as "loan limits").[1] Congress initially did so for first- and second-year undergraduate students as well as for graduate and professional students in academic year (AY) 2007-08,[2] and subsequently for all qualified undergraduate students receiving unsubsidized Stafford loans in AY 2008-09.[3] The Ensuring Continued Access to Student Loans Act of 2008 directed GAO to assess the impact of these increases in the loan limits on

---

[*] This is an edited, reformatted and augmented version of Government Accountability Office report number GAO-11-470R, dated May 2011.

tuition and other expenses and borrowing.[4] Since information was available only on the first loan limit increase, we focused on the AY 2007-08 loan limit increase, framing our study with three key questions:

1) What are the patterns in prices and undergraduate enrollment at institutions of higher education since the AY 2007-08 loan limit increases took effect?
2) To what extent did undergraduate students borrow Stafford loans at their maximum levels in AY 2007-08?
3) What are the characteristics of students in AY 2007-08 who borrowed more than the prior loan limits?

To determine patterns in college prices since the AY 2007-08 loan limit increase, we analyzed data from two U.S. Department of Education (Education) databases.[5] We used three descriptors to study postsecondary prices—tuition and required fees, total price of attendance, and net price after grants. Using the Integrated Post-Secondary Education Data System (IPEDS), we analyzed the *tuition and required fees* from AYs 1999-2000 through 2009-10 that institutions charge. Tuition and fees data are weighted by undergraduate enrollment. Using the data from the three most recent National Postsecondary Student Aid Surveys (NPSAS) (AYs 1999-2000, 2003-04, and 2007-08), we analyzed two other descriptors of price:

- total price of attendance—what a typical student would pay for tuition and required fees, books and supplies, room and board, and other personal expenses, and
- net price after grants—the total price of attendance minus all grant aid received by a typical student.

To determine patterns in undergraduate student enrollment, we used IPEDS to analyze enrollment trends from AYs 1999-2000 through 2009-10.

To determine the extent to which students were borrowing Stafford loans at their maximum levels in AY 2007-08, we used NPSAS data. For each loan type, we analyzed and compared the proportion of eligible borrowers who received their maximum amount in AY 2007-08 and AY 2003-04. To determine the characteristics of student borrowers in AY 2007-08, we analyzed available NPSAS data on institutional characteristics (geographic region and sector) and student characteristics (attendance status, dependency status, and race and ethnicity). Since the most recent NPSAS data available for our analysis is AY 2007-08, we were not able to identify any patterns after this increase in the loan limits.[6]

We determined that IPEDS and NPSAS data are sufficiently reliable for the purposes of this report by testing it for accuracy and completeness, reviewing documentation about systems used to produce the data, and interviewing agency officials. Throughout this report, all data discussed from NPSAS are statistically significant at the 95 percent confidence interval unless otherwise noted. Further, unless otherwise noted, all percentage estimates are within 5 percentage points.

We supplemented these data with interviews with officials from seven institutions of higher education that participate in federal financial aid programs. We selected this nonprobability sample to reflect a range of institutional sectors, regions, undergraduate enrollment sizes, and admission selectivity levels. We interviewed representatives from postsecondary education associations, experts, and officials from Education. In addition, we reviewed reports and other information relevant to these issues. We also reviewed relevant federal laws. Overall, these analyses are descriptive and do not necessarily indicate a linkage between increases in the loan limits and changes in tuition or borrowing.

We conducted this performance audit from October 2010 through May 2011 in accordance with generally accepted government auditing standards. Those standards require that we plan and perform the audit to obtain sufficient, appropriate evidence to provide a reasonable basis for our findings and conclusions based on our audit objectives. We believe that the evidence obtained provides a reasonable basis for our findings and conclusions on our audit objectives.

In summary, we found that:

- After the change to the Stafford loan limits beginning in AY 2007-08, the price and the numbers of undergraduate students enrolling in the nation's institutions of higher education increased at a rate generally consistent with prior years. This pattern was consistent across most institutional sectors.

- In terms of students borrowing Stafford loans, between AY 2003-04 and AY 2007-08, there was a decline in the proportion of eligible borrowers who borrowed their maximum—an amount that varies based on students' financial and personal circumstances, but is ultimately statutorily capped. These declines in borrowing were largely driven by first- and second-year students.

- A snapshot look at first- and second-year students in AY 2007-08 who borrowed more than they could have under the previous loan limits showed that they primarily attended college exclusively full-time, were dependent students, and were most commonly enrolled in public 4-year institutions. When we compared these borrowers to all other first- and second-year Stafford loan borrowers, we found similarities across many characteristics, with the exception of dependency status and institutional sector.

BACKGROUND

To help students pay for college, several forms of financial aid are available through governmental, institutional, and private sources, as shown in table 1.

Table 1. Major Aid Programs for Undergraduate Students, AYs 1999-2000, 2003-2004, and 2007-2008

(In millions of AY 2008-09 constant dollars)

	1999-2000	2003-2004	2007-2008
Federal Stafford Loans	$23,783	$30,745	$36,224
Federal Pell Grants	9,312	14,881	15,173
Federal PLUS Loans	4,244	7,299	7,955
Federal tax benefits	4,590	5,550	5,890
State grants	5,119	6,841	8,111
Institutional grants	14,240	18,170	22,160
Private loans	3,110	7,580	17,670

Source: College Board.

Note: Students generally do not need to repay grants while loans must be repaid by the student or their family. Moreover, grant aid in particular provides assistance to those whose incomes are lower, on average, than is the case with tax preferences. For more information on federal aid and tax preferences, see GAO-08-717T.

The Stafford Loan program is the largest source of federal financial aid available to postsecondary students. In AY 2009-10, 35 percent of undergraduate students participated in the program, which provided an estimated $56.1 billion dollars to eligible students through subsidized and unsubsidized loans.[7] To qualify for a subsidized loan, students must have a financial need as determined under federal law. A student's financial aid need is determined by a formula that subtracts a student's expected family contribution (EFC) and certain other estimated financial assistance from their total price of attendance.[8] In contrast to subsidized loans, students can borrow unsubsidized loans to pay for educational expenses regardless of their financial need. Depending on their educational expenses and level of financial need, a student may be eligible to receive both subsidized and unsubsidized loans, which is generally referred to as a combined loan.

The loan amount students can borrow is determined in part by their total price of attendance and financial circumstances. As shown in table 2, there is a statutory loan limit for Stafford loans that varies by a student's academic class level and dependency status (i.e., dependent or independent) and the type of loan.[9]

For unsubsidized loans, for example, independent students have higher loan limits than dependent students. Beginning with AY 2007-08, Congress raised the annual loan limits for first- and second-year undergraduate students.[10] Statutory loan limits were increased again beginning with AY 2008-09. For this subsequent increase beginning with AY 2008-09, undergraduate students in all class levels could borrow an additional $2,000 in unsubsidized or combined loans per year.

Table 2. Statutory Stafford Loan Limits before and after the Increase: Comparison of AY 2006-07 and AY 2007-08

Annual loan limits for dependent students

Class level	Academic year	Subsidized loan	Unsubsidized loan	Combined total
1st-year	2006-07	$2,625	$2,625	$2,625
	2007-08	3,500	3,500	3,500
2nd year	2006-07	3,500	3,500	3,500
	2007-08	4,500	4,500	4,500
Annual loan limits for independent students				
Class level	Academic year	Subsidized loan	Unsubsidized loan	Combined total
1st-year	2006-07	2,625	6,625	6,625
	2007-08	3,500	7,500	7,500
2nd year	2006-07	3,500	7,500	7,500
	2007-08	4,500	8,500	8,500

Source: GAO analysis of relevant federal laws.

There have been some notable changes in the availability of financial aid and in the economy since the AY 2007-08 loan limit increase. Specifically, between AY 2007-08 and AY 2009-10, the maximum award available from the Pell Grant Program rose and the Program's EFC eligibility threshold also increased, according to Education documents.[11] In addition, according to a report published by the State Higher Education Executive Officers, the recent economic recession has reduced state revenue, resulting in an overall reduction in states' support for higher education—the primary source of funding for institutional operations. At the same time, the resulting credit crisis had affected the availability of private student loans. As GAO previously reported, many of the private lenders exited the market in response to limited access to capital resulting from the credit crisis, according to select lenders, researchers, and experts. Lenders that continued their private student loans programs reportedly tightened their lending practices.[12] As these private loans declined, there was a significant increase in the total dollar amount of unsubsidized loans issued to students between AY 2007-08 and AY 2009-10.

Postsecondary Prices and Enrollment Patterns Changed Little after the AY 2007-08 Increases to Stafford Loan Limits

After the change to the Stafford loan limits took effect beginning in AY 2007-08, the price at and the numbers of undergraduate students enrolling in the nation's institutions of higher education generally continued to increase. As shown in figure 1, the tuition and required fees that most institutions charge undergraduate students generally rose at an average annual rate of about 2 to nearly 5 percent from AY 1999-2000 through AY 2009- 10.[13] The one exception to this pattern was at for-profit institutions, where the average annual rate decreased by about 4 percent since AY 2007-08.

While nearly all students are expected to pay tuition and required fees (and thus this measure is easiest to compare across sectors), this measure does not necessarily reflect the final cost that students may incur since they do not include living and other expenses or account for grant aid. When we analyzed two other measures of price—total price of attendance and net price after grants—that consider these other factors, we found that they both increased in the year this loan limit took effect, following a recent pattern of increases. (See fig. 2.)

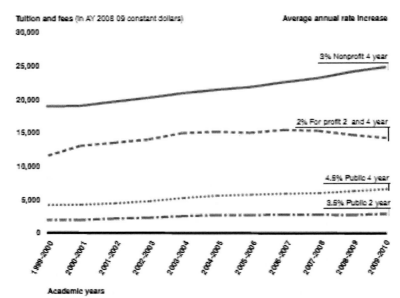

Source: GAO analysis of IPEDS data.

Figure 1. Tuition and Required Fees, AYs 1999-2000 to 2009-10, for Full-time Undergraduate Students.

According to Education data, between AY 2003-04 and AY 2007-08 the largest dollar increases occurred at for-profit institutions, where total price of attendance increased by $6,054 and net price after grant aid increased by $6,583. For both measures these increases in AY 2007-08 were preceded by decreases in AY 2003-04. For the other three sectors during this period, average total price of attendance and net price after grants increased slightly more than in the previous period. For example, at public 4-year institutions, the average total price of attendance increased by $1,280 and net price after grants increased by $928. The years chosen to measure increases in average total price of attendance and net price after grants may make a difference.

Between AYs 1999-2000 and 2007-08, for example, students attending nonprofit 4-year institutions experienced the greatest increase among the four sectors.[14] As shown in figure 2, while total price of attendance and net price after grants increased across all sectors, there can be considerable differences between these two measures of price. Grant aid, which students generally do not need to repay, lowers a student's total price of attendance and may influence the amount some students need to borrow to pay for a postsecondary education.

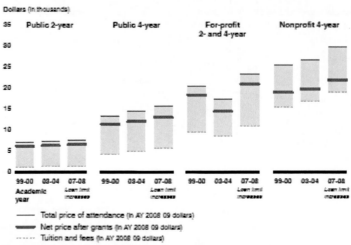

Source: GAO analysis of NPSAS data.

Note: The tuition and fees data from NPSAS displayed in this figure are lower than the tuition and fees data from IPEDS that we previously discuss because the NPSAS data includes part-time students whereas the data from IPEDS displays data only for full-time undergraduates.

Figure 2. Tuition and Fees, Total Price of Attendance, and Net Price after Grants, AYs 1999-2000, 2003-04, and 2007-08.

The average amount of grant aid received by students varies by institutional sector: students attending institutions with higher total prices of attendance generally receive more grant aid on average. In AY 2007-08, for example, students attending nonprofit 4-year and for-profit institutions had the highest average total price of attendance ($29,561 and $23,182, respectively). However, average grant aid helped to lower net price to an average of $21,688 for students at nonprofit 4-year institutions and $20,842 at for-profit institutions. Students attending public 2-year institutions had the lowest average total price of attendance ($7,495) and net price after grants ($6,487) compared with undergraduates attending other institutions in other sectors.

According to experts and administrators we interviewed at several colleges, a number of factors influence increases in prices, such as the cost of maintaining and operating facilities and providing instruction (e.g., total compensation). Moreover, several officials at public institutions said that to compensate for losses in revenue due to state budget cuts, there were tuition increases. For example, officials at one large public university system said that there were tuition increases of 30 percent in AY 2003-04 and 35 percent in AY

2009-10. None of the administrators we spoke with cited the availability of federal student aid, including increases in the loan limits, as a factor in their rationale for raising prices.

As with prices, enrollments followed an upward trend. As shown in figure 3, enrollment in institutions of higher education has been rising for more than a decade, with total enrollment at about 17.5 million students in AY 2009-10.

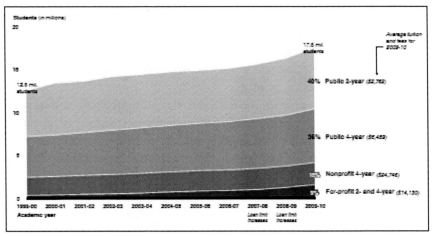

Source: GAO analysis of IPEDS data.

Figure 3. Enrollment in Degree-granting Institutions of Higher Education by Sector and Share of Students, AYs 1999-2000 to 2009-10 for Full- and Part-time Undergraduate Students

In the 3 academic years after the increase to the loan limit that took effect beginning in AY 2007-08, enrollment rose by about 2 million students (a 12 percent increase). While enrollment rose across all institutional sectors, the rate of growth varied, according to Education data. Two-year public institutions, the largest and the least expensive among the four sectors, had the greatest increases in overall student enrollment. Meanwhile, for-profit institutions had the largest enrollment increases in percentage terms, but they represent a relatively small segment of overall student enrollment. (See encl. I for information about student enrollment and sector growth rate.) For these two sectors, several administrators and experts said that the growth in enrollment is partly due to the economic recession, which increased the number of students seeking career-oriented programs offered in a flexible and convenient manner.

Proportions of Borrowers Taking Out Maximum Loan Amounts Declined After Loan Limits Increase

Between AY 2003-04 and AY 2007-08, there was a decline in the proportion of eligible Stafford loan borrowers who borrowed their maximum—an amount that varies based on their financial and personal circumstances, but is ultimately statutorily capped.[15]

For example, whereas a student with a lower total price of attendance or greater financial resources might be eligible to borrow a maximum of $600, another student with a higher total price of attendance or fewer financial resources might be eligible to borrow $3,500—the statutory limit for dependent first-year students in AY 2007-08. According to Education data, declines in maximum borrowing occurred across all three Stafford loan types, as shown in figure 4. For example, the percentage of borrowers taking out their maximum in subsidized loans—whereby the federal government pays the interest on the loan while the student is in school—dropped from 60 to 53 percent.

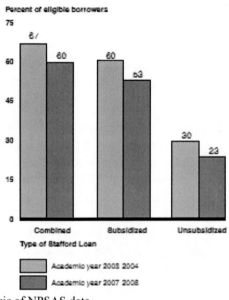

Source: GAO analysis of NPSAS data.

Figure 4. Proportion of Eligible Borrowers Who Received Their Maximum Amount in AY 2003-04 and AY 2007-08, by Stafford Loan Type.

These declines in borrowing were largely driven by first- and second-year students, who made up the majority—about 60 percent—of all borrowers. While borrowing by eligible first-year students fell by less than 10 percentage points for each loan type, borrowing by second-year students declined more sharply, ranging from a 12-point percentage drop for unsubsidized loans to a 21-point percentage drop for subsidized loans. In contrast, the proportions of third, fourth, and fifth-year borrowers who took out the maximum amounts generally showed little or no change. It is difficult to discern, with only 1 year of data available after this loan limit increase, whether this decline is part of a longer term pattern as well as what factors account for the drop. According to Education officials, a similar decline occurred after the AY 1993-94 increase in loan limits, but borrowing levels later increased. In addition, according to several college administrators we spoke with, the increased availability of grant aid for certain students from federal, state, or institutional sources may have decreased the amount they were eligible to borrow in AY 2007-08. For example, the Academic Competitiveness (AC) Grant Program began awarding grants to certain low-income first- and second-year students in AY 2006-07. The AC Grant Program will sunset at the conclusion of AY 2010-11.[16]

Students Borrowing above the Prior Loan Limits Generally Attended Public 4- Year Institutions, Enrolled in School Full-Time, and Were Dependent Students

A snapshot look at first- and second-year students in AY 2007-08 who borrowed at either (1) the new statutory limit or (2) less than the new limit (but more than they could have under the previous loan limits) showed that these two groups of borrowers shared similar key characteristics.[17] As shown in figure 5, for all loan types, students who borrowed at the new statutory limits accounted for the majority of those who borrowed more under the new loan limits.

These two groups of borrowers were similar in that they primarily attended college exclusively full-time and were dependent students.[18] Also, in general, these borrowers most commonly enrolled in public 4-year institutions and attended institutions located in the Southeast, Mid-East, and Great Lakes regions of the United States. Of note, in AY 2007-08, nearly 40 percent of all students were enrolled at public 4-year institutions; the majority of students attended institutions located in these three regions.

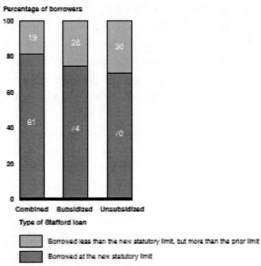

Source: GAO analysis of NPSAS data.

Figure 5. First- and Second-Year Borrowers Who Received a Loan Amount Greater than Prior Limits in AY 2007-08, by Loan Type.

When we compared the two groups of borrowers who received more than the prior loan limit to all other first- and second-year Stafford loan borrowers, we found similarities across many characteristics, with the exception of dependency status and institutional sector (see table 3 for data on combined loans). For these categories, other first- and second-year borrowers were largely independent students and attended either public 2- year or for-profit institutions in greater percentages than the students who borrowed more under the new loan limits. Moreover, the relative sizes of these three borrowing populations varied widely by loan type. For combined and subsidized loans, the majority of students borrowed at the new statutory limit. In contrast, for unsubsidized loans, the majority borrowed an amount less than the prior loan limit. (See encl. I for data on subsidized and unsubsidized loans.)

Table 3. For Combined Loans, Characteristics of First- and Second-Year Borrowers in AY 2007-08

	Percent of combined loan borrowers		
	Borrowed at the new loan limit	Borrowed less than new limit, but more than could have under prior limit	Borrowed less than the previous limit
Total population	60	14	26

	Percent of combined loan borrowers		
	Borrowed at the new loan limit	Borrowed less than new limit, but more than could have under prior limit	Borrowed less than the previous limit
Attendance status			
Exclusively full-time	73	76	52
Exclusively part-time	15	10	26
Mixed full-time and part-time	12[b]	14[b]	21
Dependency status			
Dependent	66	78	27
Independent	34	22	73
Race/ethnicity[a]			
White	62[b]	68	60 [b]
Black/African American	21[b]	15	23 [b]
Hispanic/Latino	11[b]	10 [b]	9 [b]
Institutional sector			
Public 4-year	34	43	17
Public 2-year	17	23[c]	39[c]
Nonprofit 4-year	23[b]	21[b,c]	9
For-profit 2- and 4-year	26	13	35[c]

Source: GAO analysis of NPSAS data.

[a] The column percentages for race/ethnicity do not total to 100 percent, since several categories were not included since they each accounted for 3 percent or less.

[b] For these data points, there is no statistical difference between the percentages as viewed across the columns. cFor these data points, there is no statistical difference between the percentages as viewed down the rows.

Agency Comments

We provided a draft of this letter to Education for review and comment. Education had no comments.

George A. Scott
Director, Education,
Workforce, and Income Security
Enclosure (1)

ENCLOSURE I: ADDITIONAL DATA ON THE STUDENT ENROLLMENT AS WELL AS CHARACTERISTICS OF FIRST- AND SECOND-YEAR BORROWERS IN AY 2007-08

Table 4. Student Enrollment in Degree-granting Institutions of Higher Education by Sector and by Change in Share of Overall Enrollment between Academic Years 1999-2000 and 2009-10

Sector	2007-08	2008-09	2009-2010	1999-2000 percent share of enrollment	2009-10 percent share of enrollment
Public 4-year	5,812,810	5,951,734	6,284,176	38	36
Public 2-year	6,325,103	6,640,071	7,101,444	42	40
Nonprofit 4-year	2,479,693	2,507,250	2,566,597	17	15
For-profit 2- and 4-year	995,021	1,238,327	1,585,146	3	9

Source: GAO analysis of IPEDS data.

Table 5. Characteristics of First- and Second-Year Borrowers in AY 2007-08, for Subsidized Loans

	Percent of subsidized loan borrowers		
	Borrowed at the new loan limit	Borrowed less than new limit, but more than could have under prior limit	Borrowed less than the previous limit
Total population	55	19	26
Attendance status			
Exclusively full-time	71	67	59
Exclusively part-time	16[b]	19[bc]	21[bc]
Mixed full-time and part-time	13[b]	14[bc]	20[c]
Dependency status			
Dependent	52	56	49[c]
Independent	48	44	51[c]
Race/ethnicity[a]			
White	57	62[b]	61[b]
Black/African American	23[b]	21[b]	22[b]

	Percent of subsidized loan borrowers		
	Borrowed at the new loan limit	Borrowed less than new limit, but more than could have under prior limit	Borrowed less than the previous limit
Hispanic/Latino	12^b	10^b	10^b
Institutional sector			
Public 4-year	28	35	24
Public 2-year	16	27	33^c
Nonprofit 4-year	22	18^c	11
For-profit 2- and 4-year	34^b	20^c	32^{bc}

Source: GAO analysis of NPSAS data.

[a] The column percentages for race/ethnicity do not total to 100 percent, since several categories were not included since they each accounted for 3 percent or less.

[b] For these data points, there is no statistical difference between the percentages as viewed across the columns. cFor these data points, there is no statistical difference between the percentages as viewed down the rows.

Table 6. Characteristics of First- and Second-Year Borrowers in AY 2007-08, for Unsubsidized Loans

	Percent of unsubsidized loan borrowers		
	Borrowed at the new loan limit	Borrowed less than new limit, but more than could have under prior limit	Borrowed less than the previous limit
Total population	25	11	64
Attendance status			
Exclusively full-time	74	78	59
Exclusively part-time	16	9	24
Mixed full-time and part-time	10^b	13^b	17
Dependency status			
Dependent	80	92	21
Independent	20	8	79
Race/ethnicity[a]			
White	66^b	66^b	58
Black/African American	19^b	18^b	25
Hispanic/Latino	9^b	10^b	10^b

Table 6. (Continued)

	Percent of unsubsidized loan borrowers		
	Borrowed at the new loan limit	Borrowed less than new limit, but more than could have under prior limit	Borrowed less than the previous limit
Institutional sector			
Public 4-year	40[b]	42[b]	18
Public 2-year	17[b]	19[bc]	24[b]
Nonprofit 4-year	22[bc]	21[bc]	11
For-profit 2- and 4-year	21[bc]	18[b,]	48

Source: GAO analysis of NPSAS data.

[a] The column percentages for race/ethnicity do not total to 100 percent, since several categories were not included since they each accounted for 3 percent or less.

[b] For these data points, there is no statistical difference between the percentages as viewed across the columns. cFor these data points, there is no statistical difference between the percentages as viewed down the rows.

End Notes

[1] For purposes of this report, when we refer to "loan limits," we mean annual loan limits, not aggregate limits.

[2] Pub. L. No. 109-171, § 8005, 120 Stat. 4, 158 (2006). According to our analysis of Education documents, these increases were the first changes to Stafford loan limits since AY 1993-94. For undergraduate students, these limits reflect an increase of $875 or $1,000, with the loan limits after the increase ranging from $3,500 to $8,500 depending on a student's class level, dependency status, and whether the student was receiving a subsidized or an unsubsidized loan.

[3] Pub. L. No. 110-227, § 2, 122 Stat. 740 (2008).

[4] Id. § 9, 122 Stat. 740, 748. As agreed with your staff, we did not assess the increased loan limit's impact on private loan borrowing.

[5] Our scope includes analyses of patterns in tuition, enrollment, and borrowing at institutions of higher education in the 50 states and the District of Columbia that participate in Title IV federal financial aid programs and that are degree-granting. Moreover, our scope includes four major types of institutions: 2-year public, 4-year public, 4-year nonprofit, as well as 2-year and 4-year for-profit. We grouped 2- and 4-year for-profit institutions together because about half of the institutions that classify themselves as 4-year award mainly 2-year degrees. Given that we defined our population of institutions of higher education as degree-granting, our analysis excludes less than 2-year for profit institutions that award certificates.

[6] For tuition and required fees as well as enrollment we use data from IPEDS that allowed us to study the 3 years after this increase in the loan limits (i.e., AYs 2007-08, 2008-09, and 2009-10).

[7] The federal government pays the interest on behalf of subsidized loan borrowers while the student is in school. Unsubsidized loan borrowers are responsible for all interest costs. Regardless of loan type, borrowers must be either a U.S. citizen or eligible noncitizen, and be enrolled at least half time in a degree or certificate program.

[8] The EFC represents the amount the applicant and the applicant's family can reasonably be expected to contribute toward the applicant's postsecondary education. Throughout this report, when we use the phrase "total price of attendance" in the context of the legal requirements for the Stafford Loan program, we use it to refer to "cost of attendance" as that phrase is defined in 20 U.S.C. § 1087ll.

[9] Students who are 24 years of age or older are considered independent. Younger students can be also classified as independent under certain circumstances, such if they are married or are on active military duty.

[10] Pub. L. No. 109-171, § 8005(b), 120 Stat. 4, 158 (2006).

[11] Pell Grants are need-based grants for undergraduate students who are enrolled in a degree or certificate program.

[12] GAO, Higher Education: Factors Lenders Consider in Making Lending Decisions for Private Education Loans, GAO-10-86R (Washington, D.C.: Nov. 17, 2009).

[13] The averages for tuition and fees, total price of attendance, and net price after grants are reported in AY 2008-09 constant dollars.

[14] The most recent NPSAS data for total price of attendance and net price after grants are from AY 2007-08.

[15] Because student borrowing of Stafford loans is limited by their financial need (for subsidized loans) or by their total price of attendance (for subsidized and unsubsidized loans), some students' maximum amount is the statutory limit, while for others, it is a lesser amount. Of those who received their maximum amount in AY 2007-08, 78 percent of combined borrowers, 83 percent of subsidized borrowers, and 72 percent of unsubsidized borrowers borrowed an amount equal to the statutory limits.

[16] For more information about the AC Grant Program, see GAO, Federal Student Aid: Recent Changes to Eligibility Requirements and Additional Efforts to Promote Awareness Could Increase Academic Competitiveness and SMART Grant Participation, GAO-09-343 (Washington, D.C.: Mar. 25, 2009).

[17] For example, for dependent first-year students, those who borrowed less than the new limit specifically include students who borrowed above the previous loan limit of $2,625, but less than the new AY 2007-08 limit of $3,500.

[18] The AY 2007-08 increases in Stafford loan limits for undergraduates were only applicable to students in their first- and second-year. With the higher loan limits established in AY 2007-08, certain students were able to borrow amounts greater than the previous limits.

In: Students and Stafford Loans
Editor: Daphne Rollins
ISBN: 978-1-63321-126-1
© 2014 Nova Science Publishers, Inc.

Chapter 3

BORROWING AT THE MAXIMUM: UNDERGRADUATE STAFFORD LOAN BORROWERS IN 2007–08[*]

Christina Chang Wei

In recent decades, students and families increasingly have turned to loans to help pay for postsecondary education (Draut 2009; The College Board 2009), and most undergraduates who borrow to finance their education use the federal loan programs.[1] Federal loans include Stafford, Perkins, and Parent PLUS loans, with the Stafford loan program being the largest, at a total of $35 billion borrowed by undergraduates in 2007–08 (The College Board 2009). As this report will show, in 1989–90, some 27 percent of all undergraduates had taken out a federal Stafford loan at some point during their enrollment in postsecondary education, while in 2007–08, this proportion was 46 percent. In addition, the average cumulative amount among all undergraduate borrowers was higher, even after adjusting for inflation. In 2007–08, the average cumulative Stafford loan amount was $10,300, compared with $7,200 (in constant 2007 dollars) in 1989–90 (table 1).

---

[*] This is an edited, reformatted and augmented version of a Statistics in Brief report, publication number NCES 2012-161, prepared under contract for the National Center for Education Statistics, released October 2011.

Table 1. Trends in cumulative stafford loan borrowing

Percentage of all undergraduates who had ever received federal subsidized or unsubsidized Stafford loans or Supplemental Loans for Students (SLS), and the average cumulative amount borrowed in constant 2007 dollars, by institution type and undergraduate class level: Selected years 1989–90 to 2007–08

Characteristic	1989–90		1992–93		1995–96		1999–2000		2003–04		2007–08	
	Percent who ever borrowed	Average cumulative amount	Percent who ever borrowed	Average cumulative amount	Percent who ever borrowed	Average cumulative amount	Percent who ever borrowed	Average cumulative amount	Percent who ever borrowed	Average cumulative amount	Percent who ever borrowed	Average cumulative amount
Total	26.8	$7,200	27.7	$7,500	36.2	$9,000	39.4	$10,200	42.1	$10,100	45.5	$10,300
Type of institution												
Public 4-year	28.5	7,500	32.6	7,900	47.3	10,000	50.4	11,500	52.6	11,100	52.6	11,100
Private nonprofit 4-year	39.4	8,800	41.8	9,200	55.5	10,700	59.6	11,600	62.1	11,400	61.5	11,400
Public 2-year	11.7	5,600	15.5	5,700	17.4	6,100	18.7	7,000	19.2	7,300	23.8	7,700
For-profit	70.6	6,600	53.2	6,900	67.0	7,700	81.9	9,200	85.4	9,300	91.5	10,500
Undergraduate class level												
1st-year/freshman	22.3	5,300	22.0	5,000	29.7	5,300	35.4	5,600	40.5	5,500	38.1	6,000
2nd-year/sophomore	25.3	6,700	26.5	6,100	34.5	7,700	38.3	8,900	38.9	8,700	44.3	8,900
3rd-year/junior	34.1	8,200	37.1	8,300	51.1	11,600	55.2	13,300	51.2	12,900	62.5	12,400
4th-year or higher/senior	39.2	10,800	40.3	11,300	52.7	15,300	53.6	17,800	56.4	17,700	57.7	17,300

Note: Average cumulative amounts are inflation adjusted to 2007 dollars. Cumulative loan amounts shown here include federal subsidized and unsubsidized Stafford loans as well as any Supplemental Loans for Students (SLS) received in prior years. The SLS program was an unsubsidized student loan program limited to independent students and some dependent students with special circumstances. Beginning in 1993–94, the SLS program was replaced by unsubsidized Stafford loans, which are available to both independent and dependent students regardless of need. Subsidized Stafford loans are only available to students with demonstrated financial need. Average loan amounts were calculated only for those who took out a loan. Except where indicated by the type of institution attended, this table also includes undergraduates attending more than one institution during the academic year. Estimates include students enrolled in Title IV eligible postsecondary institutions in the 50 states, the District of Columbia, and Puerto Rico.

Standard error tables are available at http://nces.ed.gov/pubsearch/ pubsinfo.asp?pubid=2012161.

Source: U.S. Department of Education, National Center for Education Statistics, 1989–90, 1992–93, 1995–96, 1999–2000, 2003–04, and 2007–08 National Postsecondary Student Aid Studies (NPSAS:90, NPSAS:93, NPSAS:96, NPSAS:2000, NPSAS:04, NPSAS:08).

Policymakers and researchers have wanted to know whether students are borrowing the maximum possible in federal (i.e., Stafford) loans before turning to alternate forms of financing such as private loans, which may have higher interest rates and less desirable repayment terms (GAO 2011; U.S. Department of Education 2008). Congress has established statutory limits on the annual and cumulative amounts that students may borrow in federal loans. Stafford loan limits vary according to the student's class year and, in the case of unsubsidized loans, the student's dependency status. Although the published annual and cumulative program limits for all students are based on class year and dependency status (i.e., the program maximum), an individual also cannot exceed his or her financial need[2] (for subsidized loans) or student budget[3] (for subsidized and unsubsidized loans combined).

To date, the analysis on the proportion taking out the maximum Stafford loan has been based on whether students take out the statutory, or *program* maximum. The percentage of students borrowing at the program maximum, however, may be an underestimate of the number of students who are actually borrowing the most they can. An individual's limit may be less than the program maximum because students are not permitted to borrow more than they need for school-related expenses, including living expenses. In the case of subsidized Stafford loans, the loan amount also cannot exceed a student's financial need, less any grants received.

Using data from the 2007–08 National Postsecondary Student Aid Study (NPSAS:08), this Statistics in Brief examines the extent to which undergraduate students borrow the maximum possible within the limits of the Stafford loan program (the program maximum) and their own financial need and student budgets (the individual maximum). Students who borrowed the maximum allowed based upon the lesser of their individual eligibility or the Stafford loan program maximum are referred to as those who "borrowed at their individual maximum." The characteristics of students borrowing at their individual maximum and the use of additional sources of financing by these students are addressed. The Brief also includes a description of how borrowing at the program maximum level changed between 1989–90 and 2007–08.

This Statistics in Brief examines students who took out the maximum Stafford loan by their dependency status and the type of institution attended. Previous analyses of borrowing have found that its use varies by these factors (Wei and Berkner 2008). When examining those who borrowed the maximum Stafford loan, the percentage that also used private loans or Parent PLUS loans was analyzed by the type of institution attended. To put the frequency and amount of borrowing in context, comparisons are made to non-borrowers and those who borrowed less than the maximum amount.

All comparisons of estimates were tested for statistical significance using the Student's t-statistic, and all differences cited are statistically significant at the $p < .05$ level.[4]

STUDY QUESTIONS

1. How has the percentage of undergraduates borrowing the *program maximum* for subsidized Stafford loans changed over the last 20 years?

2. What percentage of undergraduates with Stafford loans borrowed at their *individual maximum*, that is, the limit defined by their financial need and student budget, and how did this vary by dependency status?

3. Among undergraduates who borrowed at their *individual maximum* in total Stafford loans, what other types of financing did they use and what percentage worked full time, compared with those who borrowed less than their individual maximum and those who did not take out any Stafford loans?

Key Findings

- Among undergraduates who took out a subsidized Stafford loan between 1989–90 and 2007–08, the percentage of those borrowing the program maximum immediately decreased each time Stafford loan limits were raised, but as time went by it grew again (figure 1).

- In 2007–08, about two-thirds (66 percent) of subsidized Stafford loan borrowers took out their individual maximum in subsidized Stafford loans, as limited by the lesser of their financial need and the program maximum. About 6 in 10 (59 percent) of those who took out any Stafford loans (subsidized and unsubsidized combined) borrowed the most they could, as limited by the lesser of their total price of attendance and the program maximum (figure 2).

- Differences in the use of other types of loans (such as private loans and Parent PLUS loans) were greater between those who took out a

Stafford loan and those who did not, than between borrowers who took out the maximum allowed and those who took out less (table 3). About 30–31 percent of those who took out a Stafford loan also took out a private loan, compared with 6 percent of those who did not take out any Stafford loans. Among dependent students, about 16–18 percent of Stafford loan borrowers had parents who took out a Parent PLUS loan, compared with 0.8 percent of dependent undergraduates who did not take out any Stafford loans.

- In terms of work intensity, the percentage of students who worked full time while enrolled was lowest among Stafford loan borrowers who took out the maximum amount (26 percent), compared with those who took out less than the maximum (33 percent) and those who did not borrow (37 percent) (table 3).

1. How Has the Percentage of Undergraduates Borrowing the *Program Maximum* for Subsidized Stafford Loans Changed Over the Last 20 Years?

During the 19-year period between 1989–90 and 2007–08, the percentage of borrowers taking out the program maximum in subsidized Stafford loans varied between 41 and 51 percent, depending on the year (figure 1).[5]

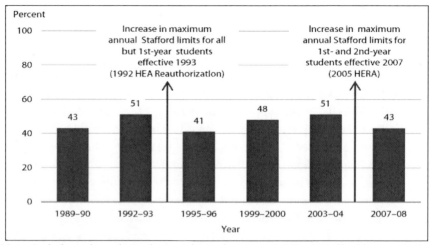

Note: Includes only undergraduates who took out a subsidized Stafford loan and who attended one institution.

Undergraduates who borrowed at the program maximum took out the maximum loan amount allowed based upon their class level. "HEA" is the Higher Education Act. "HERA" is the Higher Education Reconciliation Act. Estimates include students enrolled in Title IV eligible postsecondary institutions in the 50 states, the District of Columbia, and Puerto Rico. Standard error tables are available at http://nces.ed.gov/pubsearch/pubsinfo.asp?pubid=2012161.

Source: U.S. Department of Education, National Center for Education Statistics, 1989–90, 1992–93, 1995–96, 1999–2000, 2003–04, and 2007–08 National Postsecondary Student Aid Studies (NPSAS:90, NPSAS:93, NPSAS:96, NPSAS:2000, NPSAS:04, and NPSAS:08).

Figure 1. Borrowing at the Program Maximum.
Of undergraduates with subsidized Stafford loans, percentage who borrowed the maximum amount: Selected years 1989–90 to 2007–08.

Table 2. Stafford Program Maximum Limits
Annual and cumulative loan limits for undergraduate federal Stafford loans, by class level and dependency status: Selected years 1987–88 to 2008–09

Class level	Dependent students			Independent students		
	Sub-sidized Stafford	Unsub-sidized Stafford[1]	Combined Total	Sub-sidized Stafford	Unsub-sidized Stafford/SLS[1]	Combined Total
1987–88 to 1992–93						
1st-year	$2,625	†	$2,625	$2,625	$4,000	$6,625
2nd-year	2,625	†	2,625	2,625	4,000	6,625
3rd-, 4th-, 5th-year	4,000	†	4,000	4,000	4,000	8,000
Cumulative total	17,250	†	17,250	17,250	20,000	37,250
1993–94 to 2006–07						
1st-year	$2,625	$2,625	$2,625	$2,625	$6,625	$6,625
2nd-year	3,500	3,500	3,500	3,500	7,500	7,500
3rd, 4th, 5th-year	5,500	5,500	5,500	5,500	10,500	10,500
Cumulative total	23,000	23,000	23,000	23,000	46,000	46,000

Table 2. (Continued)

Class level	Dependent students			Independent students		
	Sub-sidized Stafford	Unsub-sidized Stafford[1]	Combined Total	Sub-sidized Stafford	Unsub-sidized Stafford/SLS[1]	Combined Total
2007–08						
1st-year	$3,500	$3,500	$3,500	$3,500	$7,500	$7,500
2nd-year	4,500	4,500	4,500	4,500	8,500	8,500
3rd-, 4th-, 5th-year	5,500	5,500	5,500	5,500	10,500	10,500
Cumulative total	23,000	23,000	23,000	23,000	46,000	46,000
2008–09						
1st-year	$3,500	$5,500	$5,500	$3,500	$9,500	$9,500
2nd-year	4,500	6,500	6,500	4,500	10,500	10,500
3rd-, 4th-, 5th-year	5,500	7,500	7,500	5,500	12,500	12,500
Cumulative total	23,000	31,000	31,000	23,000	57,500	57,500

† Not applicable.

[1] Until 1992–93, only independent students (and some dependent students with exceptional need) could take out a Supplemental Loan for Students (SLS), which was an unsubsidized student loan. Beginning in 1993–94, the SLS program was phased out and unsubsidized Stafford loans were made available to all students regardless of need.

Source: U.S. Department of Education, *The Guide to Federal Student Aid*, annual.

Congress increased the annual loan limits twice during this period, first in 1993–94 and then in 2007–08.An increase in the loan limit would then be followed by a lower percentage of students borrowing the program maximum in the subsequent year (GAO 2011). Table 2 shows the specific sub-sidized, unsubsidized, and combined Stafford loan program limits by class level and dependency status, and how they have changed over time.

In 1992–93, about one-half (51 percent) of all subsidized Stafford loan borrowers took out the program maximum (figure 1). After the reauthorization of the 1992 Higher Education Act which increased loan limits for 2nd- through 5th-year under-graduates beginning with the 1993–94academic year, those borrowing at the program maximum constituted 41 percent of all subsidized Stafford loan borrowers in 1995–96.

By 2003–04, the proportion borrowing at the program maximum had returned to about one-half (51 percent) of all subsidized Stafford loan borrowers. The enactment of the 2005 Higher Education Reconciliation Act increased loan limits again, this time for under-graduates at all levels, beginning with the 2007–08 academic year, and the percentage taking out the program maximum was 43 percent that year.

2. WHAT PERCENTAGE OF UNDERGRADUATES WITH STAFFORD LOANS BORROWED AT THEIR *INDIVIDUAL MAXIMUM*, THAT IS, THE LIMIT DEFINED BY THEIR FINANCIAL NEED AND STUDENT BUDGET, AND HOW DID THIS VARY BY DEPENDENCY STATUS?

Among all undergraduates who attended one institution and who took out a subsidized Stafford loan in 2007–08,some 44 percent borrowed at the program maximum—that is, the amount allowed for their class year and dependency status (figure 2). This estimate, however, does not mean that more than half of all borrowers could have borrowed more but did not do so. Rather, in addition to the program loan limits based on class year and dependency status, borrowers are also constrained by their financial need (for subsidized loans) or by their student budget (i.e., total price of attendance for subsidized and unsubsidized loans combined).

An individual maximum Stafford loan amount was calculated for students who took out a Stafford loan and whose class year was known. This calculation was done only for students attending one institution because student budgets were not available for those attending more than one institution. About 90 percent of all Stafford loan borrowers attended only one institution (Wei 2010a, table 5.5), allowing computation of an individual maximum Stafford loan amount for each student based upon the lesser of a student's financial need (for subsidized loans) or total student budget (for subsidized and unsubsidized loans combined) and the loan program limits. For subsidized Stafford loans, the individual maximum takes into account a student's expected family contribution (EFC) which, along with the student's total budget, determines a student's financial need. This financial need sets the limit for the amount each student can borrow from the subsidized Stafford loan program (minus any grants received), even if the program maximum is higher.

According to this analysis, some 66 percent of those taking out subsidized Stafford loans borrowed at their individual maximum in 2007–08(figure 2).In comparison, 44 percent of the same population of students took out the program maximum. Thus, about two-thirds of those taking out subsidized Stafford loans are borrowing as much as they can within the limits of their eligibility for need-based aid, a finding not apparent when considering only the percentage borrowing at the program maximum.

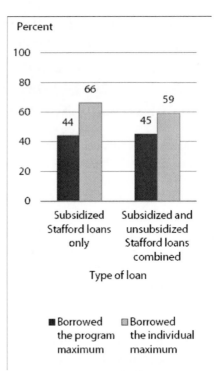

Note: Undergraduates who borrowed at the program maximum took out the annual maximum subsidized Stafford loan based on their class level and dependency status. Undergraduates who took out their individual maximum subsidized Stafford loan borrowed the maximum allowed as determined by the lesser of the program maximum or their financial need. Undergraduates who took out their individual maximum total Stafford loan (unsubsidized and subsidized loans) borrowed the maximum allowed as determined by the lesser of the program maximum or their student budget. Includes only undergraduates who took out a Stafford loan, whose class level was known, and who attended one institution. Estimates include students enrolled in Title IV eligible postsecondary institutions in the 50 states, the District of Columbia, and Puerto Rico.

Standard error tables are available at http://nces.ed.gov/pubsearch/pubsinfo.
asp?pubid=2012161.
Source: U.S. Department of Education, National Center for Education Statistics, 2007–08
National Postsecondary Student Aid Study (NPSAS:08).

Figure 2. Borrowing at the Maximum of undergraduates with Stafford loans,
percentage who borrowed the program and individual maximum amounts, by type of
Stafford loan in 2007–08.

With respect to total (subsidized and unsubsidized) Stafford borrowing,
the individual maximum cannot exceed the total price of attendance.
Unsubsidized Stafford loans are not limited by the student's financial need and
can be used to cover the EFC. Some 59 percent of those taking out any
Stafford loans (subsidized and unsubsidized combined) took out the maximum
they could, compared with45 percent who took out the program maximum.

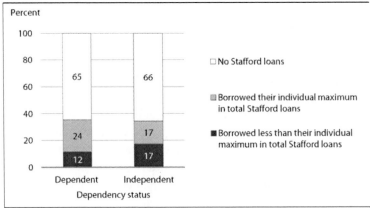

Note: Undergraduates who took out their individual maximum total Stafford loan
(unsubsidized and subsidized loans) borrowed the maximum allowed as determined by
the lesser of the program maximum or their student budget. Includes only
undergraduates who took out a Stafford loan, whose class level was known, and who
attended one institution. Estimates include students enrolled in Title IV eligible
postsecondary institutions in the 50 states, the District of Columbia, and Puerto Rico.
Standard error tables are available at http://nces.ed.gov/pubsearch/pubsinfo.
asp?pubid=2012161.
Source: U.S. Department of Education, National Center for Education Statistics, 2007–08
National Postsecondary Student Aid Study (NPSAS:08).

Figure 3. Stafford Loan Status
Percentage distribution of undergraduates' Stafford loan status, by dependency status
in 2007–08.

Independent students have higher total Stafford loan limits than do dependent students (table 2). Subject to this higher total loan limit, relatively fewer independent students than dependent students reached their individual maximum for total Stafford borrowing. While about one-fourth (24percent) of all dependent students borrowed at their individual maximum in Stafford loans, only 17 percent of independent students did so (figure 3).

3. AMONG UNDERGRADUATES WHO BORROWED AT THEIR INDIVIDUAL MAXIMUM IN TOTAL STAFFORD LOANS, WHAT OTHER TYPES OF FINANCING DID THEY USE AND WHAT PERCENTAGE WORKED FULL TIME, COMPARED TO THOSE WHO BORROWED LESS THAN THEIR INDIVIDUAL MAXIMUM AND THOSE WHO DID NOT TAKE OUT ANY STAFFORD LOANS?

About three-fourths of all undergraduates who took out a Stafford loan—regardless of whether they borrowed at their individual maximum or less than their individual maximum—had received grants (about 73 percent), compared with 41 percent of those who did not take out any Stafford loans at all (table 3). Similarly, when analyzing the use of other types of financing (such as private loans and Parent PLUS loans) the differences in the percentages of those using other types of loans were greatest between those who took out a Stafford loan and those who did not, rather than between those who borrowed the maximum allowed and those who borrowed less.

While nearly one-third (30–31 percent) of students who took out a Stafford loan also took out private loans, about 6 percent of those who did not take out any Stafford loans also took out a private loan. Among dependent undergraduates, 18 percent of those who borrowed at their individual maximum in total Stafford loans had parents who took out a Parent PLUS loan, compared with 16 percent of those who borrowed less than their individual maximum and about 1 percent of those who did not take out any Stafford loans.

Students attending private institutions face a higher average tuition and student budget than do students in public institutions (Wei 2010c) and this is reflected in the relatively higher proportion of students in private institutions taking out private loans, among those who had already borrowed the maximum Stafford loan (figures 4 and 5). Furthermore, relatively more dependent students than independent students took out private loans, reflecting the lower total Stafford loan limits among dependent students.

Table 3. All Undergraduates, Non-Stafford Loan Borrowers, and Stafford Loan Borrowers
Percentage distribution of undergraduates by demographic, enrollment, and financial aid characteristics: 2007–08

Characteristic	Total undergraduates[1]	No Stafford loans[1]	Borrowed less than their individual maximum in total Stafford loans[2]	Borrowed their individual maximum in total Stafford loans[2]
Total	**100.0**	**100.0**	**100.0**	**100.0**
Dependency status				
Dependent	53.0	51.9	43.4	61.8
Independent	47.0	48.1	56.6	38.2
Unmarried, no dependents[3]	15.7	15.8	18.8	13.4
Married, no dependents	5.9	6.8	5.2	3.6
Unmarried, with dependents[3]	13.4	12.6	18.6	12.8
Married, with dependents	12.0	12.9	14.0	8.3
Income by dependency status				
Dependent income				
Lowest 25 percent	25.0	23.9	26.0	27.7
Lower middle 25 percent	25.0	23.9	28.6	26.2
Higher middle 25 percent	25.0	24.5	27.1	25.5
Highest 25 percent	25.0	27.7	18.3	20.7
Independent income				
Lowest 25 percent	25.0	22.2	29.7	31.8
Lower middle 25 percent	25.0	22.5	29.9	30.3
Higher middle 25 percent	25.0	25.0	25.2	24.5
Highest 25 percent	25.0	30.3	15.2	13.4
Type of institution				
Public 4-year	32.1	28.5	37.8	39.7

Table 3. (Continued)

Characteristic	Total undergraduates[1]	No Stafford loans[1]	Borrowed less than their individual maximum in total Stafford loans[2]	Borrowed their individual maximum in total Stafford loans[2]
Private nonprofit 4-year	14.2	10.0	18.9	25.0
Public 2-year	43.8	59.7	18.7	9.4
For-profit	9.9	1.8	24.6	25.8
Attendance status				
Full-time, full-year	37.8	29.2	51.7	58.0
Part-time or part-year	62.2	70.8	48.3	42.0
Grant status				
Received any grants	51.7	40.8	72.0	73.9
Did not receive any grants	48.3	59.2	28.0	26.1
Private loan status				
Took out any private loans	14.2	5.6	30.3	30.7
Did not take out any private loans	85.8	94.4	69.7	69.3
Parent PLUS loans[4]				
Took out any Parent PLUS loans	7.1	0.8	15.8	17.9
Did not take out any Parent PLUS loans	92.9	99.2	84.2	82.1
Employment status				
Not employed	21.0	20.4	20.9	23.5
Employed part time	45.0	42.9	46.1	50.7
Employed full time	33.9	36.7	33.0	25.7
Dependent student employment status				
Not employed	23.8	23.7	22.9	24.9
Employed part time	58.4	56.8	61.3	61.4
Employed full time	17.8	19.6	15.8	13.8
Independent student employment status				
Not employed	17.9	16.9	19.4	21.4
Employed part time	30.0	27.9	34.4	33.5
Employed full time	52.1	55.3	46.2	45.1

[1] Includes those attending more than one institution except where institution type is shown separately.

[2] Includes only those who took out a Stafford loan, whose class level was known, and who attended one institution.

[3] "Unmarried" includes separated students.

[4] Dependent students only.

Note: Undergraduates who took out their individual maximum total Stafford loan (unsubsidized and subsidized loans combined) borrowed the maximum allowed as determined by the lesser of the program maximum or their student budget. For dependent students, income categories were based upon the distribution of parents' annual income in 2006. "Lowest 25 percent" is less than $36,150, including those with no income; "Lower middle 25 percent" is $36,150–$66,621; "Higher middle 25 percent" is $66,622–$104,586; "Highest 25 percent" is $104,587 or more. For independent students, income categories were based upon the distribution of student's own income and his or her spouse's income, if married. "Lowest 25 percent" is less than $11,009, including those with no income; "Lower middle 25 percent" is $11,009–$25,978; "higher middle 25 percent" is $25,979–$48,429; "Highest 25 percent" is $48,430 or more. "Attendance status" does not include students attending multiple institutions. Grants include scholarships and tuition waivers. Parent PLUS loans are only available to the parents of dependent students. Estimates include students enrolled in Title IV eligible postsecondary institutions in the 50 states, the District of Columbia, and Puerto Rico. Detail may not sum to totals because of rounding. Standard error tables are available at http://nces.ed.gov/pubsearch/ pubsinfo.asp?pubid=2012161.

Source: U.S. Department of Education, National Center for Education Statistics, 2007–08 National Postsecondary Student Aid Study (NPSAS:08).

PARENT PLUS LOANS VERSUS PRIVATE LOANS

Federal aid policy assumes that parents have primary responsibility for a dependent student's educational expenses. The federally guaranteed Parent PLUS loan program was established to aid these families. Like all other federally guaranteed student loans, the Parent PLUS loan has better repayment terms than most private loans, but unlike all other student loans, repayment is the parents' obligation. Under federal regulations, therefore, dependent students whose parents cannot meet the creditworthiness criteria for a Parent PLUS loan are allowed to borrow unsubsidized Stafford loans up to the independent student maximum. If parents are eligible for but do not take out a Parent PLUS loan, the other common alternative for dependent students is to take out a private student loan.

A dependent student's price of attendance is also associated with the use of Parent PLUS loans. Undergraduates at public 2-year institutions had the lowest average student budget (Wei2010c). They also had the smallest proportion of dependent students whose parents took out a Parent PLUS loan

(3 percent) when compared with dependent students at other institutions (18–21 percent)—among those who also took out the maximum Stafford loan.

At all types of institutions, dependent students took out private loans at higher rates than their parents took out Parent Plus loans (17 percent to 48 percent had private loans, while 3 percent to 21 percent had Parent PLUS loans) among those who borrowed the maximum Stafford loan (figure 4)—even though private loans usually have repayment terms that are less desirable (U.S. Department of Education 2008).

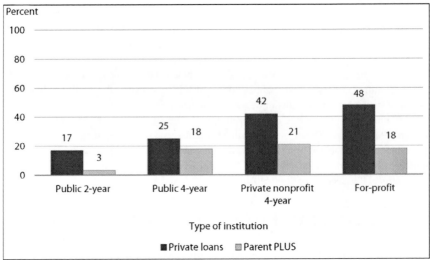

Note: Includes only dependent undergraduates whose class level was known, who attended one institution, and who took out a Stafford loan at their individual maximum. Dependent undergraduates who took out their individual maximum total Stafford loan (unsubsidized and subsidized loans) borrowed the maximum allowed as determined by the lesser of the program maximum or their student budget. Parent PLUS loans are only available to the parents of dependent students. Estimates include students enrolled in Title IV eligible postsecondary institutions in the 50 states, the District of Columbia, and Puerto Rico. Standard error tables are available at http://nces.ed.gov/pubsearch/pubsinfo.asp?pubid=2012161.

Source: U.S. Department of Education, National Center for Education Statistics, 2007–08 National Postsecondary Student Aid Study (NPSAS:08).

Figure 4. Additional borrowing among dependent students
Of dependent undergraduates who took out their individual maximum total Stafford loan, percentages who also took out private loans or whose parents took out a Parent PLUS loan: 2007–08.

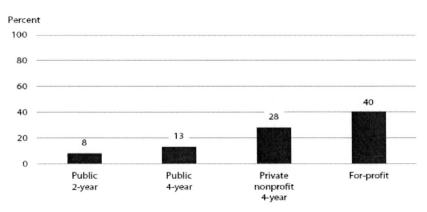

Note: Includes only independent undergraduates whose class level was known, who attended one institution, and who took out a Stafford loan at their individual maximum. Independent undergraduates who took out their individual maximum total Stafford loan (unsubsidized and subsidized loans) borrowed the maximum allowed as determined by the lesser of the program maximum or their student budget. Estimates include students enrolled in Title IV eligible postsecondary institutions in the 50 states, the District of Columbia, and Puerto Rico. Standard error tables are available at http://nces.ed.gov/pubsearch/pubsinfo.asp?pubid=2012161.
Source: U.S. Department of Education, National Center for Education Statistics, 2007–08 National Postsecondary Student Aid Study (NPSAS:08).

Figure 5. Private Loan Borrowing among Independent Students
Of independent undergraduates who took out their individual maximum total Stafford loan, percentage who also took out a private loan, by type of institution: 2007–08.

Undergraduates who take out student loans often still need additional funds to cover their expenses, so it is not surprising that Stafford loan borrowers used other sources of financing at higher rates than undergraduates who did not borrow. However, the opposite pattern emerged when employment was taken into account. When compared with those who borrowed less than the maximum and those who did not take out a Stafford loan, work intensity while enrolled was lowest among those who borrowed at the maximum in Stafford loans(table 3).About one-fourth (26 percent) of those who borrowed the maximum Stafford loan worked full time while enrolled compared with about one-third (33 percent) of those who took out less than the maximum Stafford loan and 37percent of those who did not take out any Stafford loans.

FIND OUT MORE

For questions about content or to order additional copies of this Statistics in Brief or view this report online, go to: http://nces.ed.gov/pubsearch/ pubsinfo.asp?pubid=2012161

More detailed information on 2007–08 undergraduate Stafford loan borrowing can be found in the following Web Tables produced by the National Center for Education Statistics (NCES) using NPSAS:08 data. Included are estimates of Stafford loan borrowing from 1989–90 to 2007–08 based on six separate administrations of NPSAS.

Web Tables—Trends in Undergraduate Stafford Loan Borrowing: 1989–90 to 2007–08 (NCES 2010-183). http://nces.ed.gov/pubsearch/ pubsinfo.asp?pubid=2010183

Readers also may be interested in the following NCES products related to topics covered in this Statistics in Brief:

Web Tables—Profile of Undergraduate Students in U.S. Postsecondary Institutions: 2007–08 (NCES 2010-205). http://nces.ed.gov/pubsearch/ pubsinfo.asp?pubid= 2010205

Web Tables—Student Financing of Undergraduate Education: 2007–08 (NCES 2010-162). http://nces.ed.gov/pubsearch/pubsinfo.asp?pubid= 2010162

Technical Notes

Survey Methodology

The estimates provided in this Statistics in Brief are based on data collected through the 1989–90, 1992–93, 1995–96, 1999–2000, 2003–04, and2007–08 National Postsecondary Student Aid Studies (NPSAS:90, NPSAS:93, NPSAS:96, NPSAS:2000, NPSAS:04, and NPSAS:08). NPSAS covers broad topics concerning student enrollment in post-secondary education and how students and their families finance their education. In 1990, 1993, 1996, and 2000, students provided data through surveys administered over the telephone, and in 2004 and 2008, through surveys administered over the Internet or by telephone. In addition to student responses, data were collected from the institutions that sampled students attended and other relevant databases, including U.S. Department of Education records on student loan and grant programs and student financial aid applications. NPSAS has been conducted every 3 to 4 years since 1986–87. The NPSAS:90, NPSAS:93, NPSAS:96, NPSAS:2000, NPSAS:04, and NPSAS:08 target population includes students enrolled in postsecondary institutions in the United States and Puerto Rico at any time between July 1st and June 30th of the survey year.[6] In NPSAS:2000, NPSAS:04, and NPSAS:08, the population was also limited to students enrolled in Title IV institutions.[7] Table A-1 provides the sizes of the undergraduate and graduate components of the target population.

Table A-1. Target populations, number of participating institutions, and unweighted number of study members: NPSAS:90 to NPSAS:08

NPSAS year	Sampling frame	Target undergraduate population (in millions)	Target graduate population (in millions)	Participating Institutions	Number of undergraduate study members	Number of graduate study members
NPSAS:90	1987–88 IPEDS	16.3	1.8	1,100	46,800	14,300
NPSAS:93	1990–91 IPEDS	18.5	2.7	1,100	52,700	13,400
NPSAS:96[1]	1993–94 IPEDS	16.7	2.8	800	41,500	7,000
NPSAS:2000	1998–99 IPEDS[2]	16.6	2.7	1,000	49,900	11,800
NPSAS:04	2000–01 IPEDS	19.1	2.8	1,400	79,900	10,900
NPSAS:08	2004–05 IPEDS	20.9	3.5	1,700	113,500	14,200

[1] NPSAS:96 was the last survey to include institutions that were not eligible for Title IV funds.

[2] Supplemented by 1996–97 IPEDS Completions file because NPSAS:2000 served as a base year for Baccalaureate and Beyond Longitudinal Study (B&B).

Source: Cominole, M.B., Siegel, P.H., Dudley, K., Roe, D., and Gilligan, T. (2006). *2004 National Postsecondary Student Aid Study (NPSAS:04) Full-Scale Methodology Report* (NCES 2006-180). National Center for Education Statistics, Institute of Education Sciences, U.S. Department of Education. Washington, DC. Riccobono, J.A., Cominole, M.B., Siegel, P.H., Gabel, T.J., Link, M.W., and Berkner L.K. (2001). *National Postsecondary Student Aid Study, 1999–2000 (NPSAS:2000) Methodology Report* (NCES 2002-152). National Center for Education Statistics, U.S. Department of Education. Washington, DC. Cominole, M.B., Riccobono, J.A., Siegel, P.H., and

Caves, L. (2010). *2007–08 National Postsecondary Student Aid Study (NPSAS:08) Full-scale Methodology Report* (NCES 2011-188). National Center for Education Statistics, Institute of Education Sciences, U.S. Department of Education. Washington, DC. Riccobono, J.A., Whitmore, R.W., Gabel, T.J., Traccarella, M.A., Pratt, D.J., and Berkner, L.K. (1997). *National Postsecondary Student Aid Study, 1995–96 (NPSAS:96) Methodology Report* (NCES 98-073). National Center for Education Statistics, U.S. Department of Education. Washington, DC. Shepard, J. (1992). *Methodology Report for the 1990 National Postsecondary Student Aid Study* (NCES 92-080). National Center for Education Statistics, U.S. Department of Education. Washington, DC. Loft, J.D., Riccobono, J.A., Whitmore, R.W., Fitzgerald, R.A., and Berkner, L.K., (1995). *Methodology Report for the National Postsecondary Student Aid Study, 1992–93* (NCES 95-211). National Center for Education Statistics, U.S. Department of Education. Washington, DC.

Table A-2. Weighted response rates for NPSAS surveys: NPSAS:90 to NPSAS:08

Component	Institution list participation rate	Student response rate	Overall[1]
NPSAS:90			
Student survey (analysis file[2])	86	84	72
Student survey (student interview)	86	76	65
NPSAS:93			
Student survey (analysis file[2])	88	75	66
Student survey (student interview)	88	67	59
NPSAS:96			
Student survey (analysis file[2])	91	93	88
Student survey (student interview)	91	76	70
NPSAS:2000			
Student survey (analysis file[2])	91	97	89
Student survey (student interview)	91	72	66
NPSAS:04			
Student survey (analysis file[2])	80	91	72
Student survey (student interview)	80	71	56
NPSAS:08			
Student survey (analysis file[2])	90	96	86
Student survey (student interview)	90	71	64

[1] Institution list participation rate times student response rate.
[2] NPSAS analysis file contains analytic variables derived from all NPSAS data sources (including institutional records and external data sources) as well as selected direct student interview variables.

Note: The student interview response rates for NPSAS:96 and NPSAS:2000 are for telephone interviews only. The response rates for student interviews in NPSAS:04 and NPSAS:08 include all interview modes (self-administered web-based, telephone, and in-person interviews).

Source: Riccobono, J.A., Whitmore, R.W., Gabel, T.J., Traccarella, M.A., Pratt, D.J., and Berkner, L.K. (1997). *National Post-secondary Student Aid Study, 1995–96 (NPSAS:96) Methodology Report* (NCES 98-073). National Center for Education Statistics, U.S. Department of Education. Washington, DC. Thurgood, L., Walter, E., Carter, G., Henn, S., Huang, G., Nooter, D., Smith, W., Cash, R.W., and Salvucci, S. (2003). *NCES Handbook of Survey Methods* (NCES 2003-603). National Center for Education Statistics, U.S. Department of Education. Washington, DC. Burns, S., Wang, X., and Henning, A. (Eds.) (2011). *NCES Handbook of Survey Methods* (NCES 2011-609). National Center for Education Statistics, Institute of Education Sciences, U.S. Department of Education. Washington, DC.

Table A-1 also lists the institution sampling frames for NPSAS:90, NPSAS:93, NPSAS:96, NPSAS:2000, NPSAS:04, and NPSAS:08, which were constructed from contemporary Institutional Characteristics, Fall Enrollment, and Completions files of the Integrated Postsecondary Education Data System (IPEDS).

The sampling design consisted of first selecting eligible institutions, then selecting students from these institutions. Institutions were selected with probabilities proportional to a composite measure of size based on expected enrollment during the survey year. Table A-1 includes the approximate number of institutions participating in each of the survey years, and the corresponding weighted institution unit response rates. In NPSAS:08, eligible sampled students were defined as study respondents if at least 11 key data elements were available from any data source. Similar definitions of study respondents were developed for each of the earlier NPSAS administrations. See the methodology reports listed at the end of this section for detailed descriptions of these definitions.

The approximate number of undergraduates and graduate students who were study respondents in each survey year is also reported in table A-1.

Table A-2 provides a summary of weighted response rates across NPSAS administrations. There are several types of participation/coverage rates in NPSAS. For the student record abstraction phase of the study (referred to as computer-assisted data entry or CADE), institution completion rates vary across different types of institutions and depend on the method of data submission (field-CADE, self-CADE, and data-CADE).

Overall student-level CADE completion rates, i.e., the percentage of NPSAS-eligible sample members for whom a completed CADE record was obtained, are reported in table A-2 as "Student survey (analysis file)." This table also contains weighted response rates to the student interview, which includes respondents who completed either a full or partial "Student survey (student interview)."

Estimates were weighted to adjust for the unequal probability of selection into the sample and for nonresponse.

Two broad categories of error occur in estimates generated from surveys: sampling and nonsampling errors. Sampling errors occur when observations are based on samples rather than on entire populations. The standard error of a sample statistic is a measure of the variation due to sampling and indicates the precision of the statistic.

The complex sampling design used in NPSAS must be taken into account when calculating variance estimates such as standard errors. NCES's online PowerStats, which generated the estimates in this report, use the balanced repeated replication (BRR) and Jackknife II (JK2) methods to adjust variance estimation for the complex sample design.

Nonsampling errors can be attributed to several sources: incomplete information about all respondents (e.g., some students or institutions refused to participate, or students participated but answered only certain items); differences among respondents in question interpretation; inability or unwillingness to give correct information; mistakes in recording or coding data; and other errors of collecting, processing, sampling, and imputing missing data.

VARIABLES USED

All estimates presented in this Statistics in Brief were produced using PowerStats, a web-based software application that allows users to generate tables for many of the postsecondary surveys conducted by NCES. The variables used in this Brief are listed below. Visit the NCES DataLab website (http://nces.ed.gov/datalab) to view detailed information on how these variables were constructed and their sources. Under *Detailed Information About PowerStats Variables, NPSAS Undergraduates: 2008*, click *by subject* or *by variable* name.

The program files that generated the statistics presented in this Brief can be found at http://nces.ed.gov/pubsearch/pubs info.asp?pubid=2012161.

Label	Name
NPSAS:08	
Attendance pattern	ATTNSTAT
Dependency status	DEPEND
Dependency and marital status	DEPEND5B
Institution type	SECTOR4
Maximum subsidized Stafford loan amount	STAFCT1
Parent PLUS loan total	PLUSAMT
Private loans	PRIVLOAN
Stafford individual subsidized maximum	ESUBMX2
Stafford individual total maximum	ETOTMX2
Stafford statutory subsidized maximum	STSUBMX
Stafford statutory total maximum	STTOTMX
Stafford subsidized loan	STAFSUB
Stafford total subsidized unsubsidized	STAFFAMT
Total grants	TOTGRT
Total income—parents and independent	CINCOME
Work intensity	JOBENR2
NPSAS:04	
Stafford subsidized loan	STAFSUB
NPSAS:2000	
Stafford subsidized loan	STAFSUB
NPSAS:96	
Stafford subsidized loan	STAFSUB
NPSAS:93	
Stafford subsidized loan	STAFFR
NPSAS:90	
Stafford subsidized loan	STAFFR

For more information on NPSAS:90, NPSAS:93, NPSAS:96, NPSAS:2000, NPSAS:04, and NPSAS:08 methodology, see the following reports:

- *Methodology Report for the 1990 National Postsecondary Student Aid Study* (http://nces.ed.gov/pubsearch/pubsinfo.asp?pubid=92080)
- *Methodology Report for the 1993 National Postsecondary Student Aid Study* (http://nces.ed.gov/pubsearch/pubsinfo.asp?pubid=95211)
- *National Postsecondary Student Aid Study, 1995–96 (NPSAS:96) Methodology Report* (http://nces.ed.gov/pubsearch/pubsinfo.asp?pubid=98073)
- *National Postsecondary Student Aid Study 1999–2000 (NPSAS:2000) Methodology Report* (http://nces.ed. gov/pubsearch/pubsinfo.asp?pubid=2002152)
- *2004 National Postsecondary Student Aid Study (NPSAS:04) Full-scale Methodology Report* (http://nces.ed.gov/pubsearch/pubsinfo.asp?pubid=2006180)
- *2007–08 National Postsecondary Student Aid Study (NPSAS:08) Full-scale Methodology Report* (http://nces.ed.gov/pubsearch/pubs info.asp?pubid=2011188)

Item Response Rates

NCES Statistical Standard 4-4-1 states that "any survey stage of data collection with a unit or item response rate less than 85 percent must be evaluated for the potential magnitude of nonresponse bias before the data or any analysis using the data may be released" (U.S. Department of Education 2002). In the case of NPSAS:08, this means that nonresponse bias analysis could be required at any of three levels: (a) institutions, (b) study respondents, or (c) items. Because the institutional and study respondent response rates were 90 and 96 percent, respectively, nonresponse bias analysis was not required at those levels.

The student interview response rate, however, was 71 percent, and therefore nonresponse bias analysis was required for those variables based in whole or in part on student interviews. In this report, seven variables required nonresponse bias analysis. Those variables and their respective weighted item response rates are as follows: CINCOME (51 percent), DEPEND5B (81 percent), ESUBMX2 (16 percent), ETOTMX2 (29 percent), JOBENR (54 percent), PRIVLOAN (67 percent), and TOTGRT (61 percent). For each of these variables, nonresponse bias analyses were conducted to determine whether respondents and nonrespondents differed on the following characteristics: institution sector, region, and total enrollment; student type, gender, and age group; whether the student had Free Application for Federal Student Aid (FAFSA) data, was a federal aid recipient, was a Pell Grant recipient, or borrowed a Stafford loan; and the amount, if any, of a student's Pell Grant or Stafford loan. Differences between respondents and nonrespondents on these variables were tested for statistical significance at the 5 percent level.

Nonresponse bias analyses of the variables in this report with response rates less than 85 percent indicated that respondents differed from nonrespondents on 71 to 80 percent of the characteristics analyzed, indicating that there may be bias in these estimates. Any bias due to nonresponse, however, is based upon responses prior to stochastic imputation. The potential for bias in these estimates is tempered by two factors.

First, potential bias may have been reduced due to imputation. Because imputation procedures are designed specifically to identify donors with similar characteristics to those with missing data, the imputation is assumed to reduce bias. While item-level bias before imputation is measurable, such bias after imputation is not, so whether the imputation affected the bias cannot be directly evaluated. Therefore, the item estimates before and after imputation were compared to determine whether the imputation changed the biased estimate, thus suggesting a reduction in bias.

For continuous variables, the difference between the mean before imputation and the mean after imputation was estimated. For categorical variables, the estimated difference was computed for each of the categories as the percentage of students in that category before imputation minus the percentage of students in that category after imputation. These estimated differences were tested for statistical significance at the 5 percent level. A significant difference in the item means after imputation implies a reduction in bias due to imputation. A nonsignificant difference suggests that imputation may not have reduced bias, that the sample size was too small to detect a significant difference, or that there was little bias to be reduced. Statistical tests of the differences between the means before and after imputation for five variables (DEPEND5B, ETOTMX2, JOBENR, PRIVLOAN, and TOTGRT) were significant, indicating that the nonresponse bias was reduced through imputation. Tests were not significant for the remainder of the variables.

Second, for some composite variables, some components from which the composites are constructed constitute a small proportion of the composite, attenuating the potential bias introduced by nonresponse to the component. For example, most of the components of TOTGRT (total amount of all grants received) were obtained from federal databases and institutional records and have very high response rates. Some components of TOTGRT, however, are types of grants that are often disbursed directly to students and not through institutions (e.g., employer aid). Because the primary source of information about such types of aid is the student interview, these variables were missing for interview nonrespondents and, therefore, reduce the response rate of the variable overall.

In the case of missing information from the student interview, values were stochastically imputed and the imputed values used to construct the composite variables. In the example cited above, employer aid was received by relatively few students and was a small component of the total. For example, 52 percent of all undergraduates received any grants (TOTGRT), and the average among all undergraduates was $2,500. In comparison, 8 percent received any employer aid (EMPLYAM3), a component of TOTGRT, with an average among all undergraduates of $200. In cases such as these, despite the low response rate of the component, any bias it contributes is likely to be minimal.

For more detailed information on non-response bias analysis and an overview of the survey methodology, see *2007–08 National Postsecondary Student Aid Study (NPSAS:08) Full-scale Methodology Report* (http://nces.ed.gov/pubsearch/ pubsinfo.asp?pubid=2011188).

Statistical Procedures

Comparisons of means and proportions were tested using t statistic. Differences between estimates were tested against the probability of a Type I error[8] or significance level. The statistical significance of each comparison was determined by calculating the Student's t value for the difference between each pair of means or proportions and comparing the t value with published tables of significance levels for two-tailed hypothesis testing. Student's t values were computed to test differences between independent estimates using the following formula:

$$t = \frac{E_1 - E_2}{\sqrt{se_1^2 + se_2^2}}$$

where E_1 and E_2 are the estimates to be compared and se_1 and se_2 are their corresponding standard errors.

There are hazards in reporting statistical tests for each comparison. First, comparisons based on large t statistics may appear to merit special attention. This can be misleading since the magnitude of the t statistic is related not only to the observed differences in means or percentages but also to the number of respondents in the specific categories used for comparison. Hence, a small difference compared across a large number of respondents would produce a large (and thus possibly statistically significant) *t* statistic.

A second hazard in reporting statistical tests is the possibility that one can report a "false positive" or Type I error. Statistical tests are designed to limit the risk of this type of error using a value denoted by alpha. The alpha level of .05 was selected for findings in this report and ensures that a difference of a certain magnitude or larger would be produced when there was no actual difference between the quantities in the underlying population no more than 1 time out of 20.[9] When analysts test hypotheses that show alpha values at the .05 level or smaller, they reject the null hypothesis that there is no difference between the two quantities. Failing to reject a null hypothesis (i.e., detect a difference), however, does not imply the values are the same or equivalent.

REFERENCES

The College Board. (2009). *Trends in Student Aid, 2009*. Washington, DC: Author.

Draut, T. (2009). Debt-for-Diploma System. *The New England Journal of Higher Education, 23*, 31–32.

Government Accountability Office (GAO). (2011, May 25). *Federal Student Loans; Patterns in Tuition, Enrollment, and Federal Stafford Loan Borrowing Up to the 2007–08 Loan Limit Increase* (GAO-11-470R). Washington, DC: Author.

U.S. Department of Education. (2002). *NCES Statistical Standards* (NCES 2003-601). National Center for Education Statistics, U.S. Department of Education. Washington, DC.

U.S. Department of Education, Federal Student Aid, Students Channel (2008). *Your Federal Student Loans: Learn the Basics and Manage Your Debt*. Washington, DC: Author.

Wei, C. (2010a). *Web Tables—Student Financing of Undergraduate Education:2007–08* (NCES 2010-162). National Center for Education Statistics, Institute of Education Sciences, U.S. Department of Education. Washington, DC.

Wei, C. (2010b). *Web Tables—Trends in Undergraduate Stafford Loan Borrowing: 1989–90 to 2007–08* (NCES 2010-183). National Center for Education Statistics, Institute of Education Sciences, U.S. Department of Education. Washington, DC.

Wei, C. (2010c). *What Is the Price of College? Total, Net, and Out-of-Pocket Prices in 2007–08* (NCES 2011-175). National Center for Education Statistics, Institute of Education Sciences, U.S. Department of Education. Washington, DC.

Wei, C., and Berkner, L. (2008). *Trends in Undergraduate Borrowing II: Federal Student Loans in 1995–96, 1999–2000, and 2003–04* (NCES 2008-179REV). National Center for Education Statistics, Institute of Education Sciences, U.S. Department of Education. Washington, DC.

End Notes

[1] In 2007–08, some 39 percent of all undergraduates took out a student loan to finance their education, with 35 percent taking out any federal Stafford loans, 30 percent taking out subsidized Stafford loans, and 22 percent with unsubsidized Stafford loans (Wei 2010a, table 3.1-a, and Wei 2010b, tables 1.1, 1.2, and 1.3).

[2] Financial need for federal financial aid purposes is defined as the student budget less any expected family contribution (EFC) calculated using federal need analysis methodology. Federal need analysis takes into consideration the family income and assets dependent students and for independent students); family size; number of family members in college; and other related factors.

[3] The student budget is also known as the total price of attendance and includes all expenses necessary for attending a postsecondary institution. A student budget is composed of tuition and fees, books and supplies, housing, food, and transportation, and personal or miscellaneous expenses.

[4] While z-tests could have been used, the results of z-tests and t-tests converge with larger cell sizes, making t-tests an appropriate choice. No adjustments for multiple comparisons were made. The standard errors for the estimates can be found at http://nces.ed.gov/pubsearch/pubsinfo.asp?pubid=2012161.

[5] Only subsidized Stafford loans are included in this analysis because unsubsidized Stafford loans were not available in 1989–90 and 1992–93, and the same limits for subsidized loans apply to both dependent and independent students in each survey year. Readers should also note that although t-tests were used to test differences in the percentage of those borrowing at the maximum, no time series analysis was conducted for this report.

[6] The target population of students was limited to those enrolled in an academic program, at least one course for credit that could be applied toward an academic degree, or an occupational or vocational program requiring at least 3 months or 300 clock hours of instruction to receive a degree, certificate, or other formal award. The target population excluded students who were also enrolled in high school or a high school completion (e.g., GED preparation) program.

[7] "Title IV institutions" refers to institutions eligible to participate in federal financial aid programs under Title IV of the Higher Education Act.

[8] A Type I error occurs when one concludes that a difference observed in a sample reflects a true difference in the population from which the sample was drawn, when no such difference is present.

[9] No adjustments were made for multiple comparisons.

INDEX